Butterflies
of FLORIDA
FIELD GUIDE

by Jaret C. Daniels

Adventure Publications
Cambridge, Minnesota

ACKNOWLEDGEMENTS:

I would like to thank Thomas C. Emmel, Ph.D., a distinguished professor and lepidopterist, for his continued guidance in my career and personal endeavors. And thanks to my wife, Stephanie, for her unending patience dealing with the countless number of caterpillars, butterflies and associated plant material that happens to always find a way into our home.

Photo credits by photographer and page number:
Cover photo: Queen by Jaret C. Daniels
Rick and Nora Bowers/BowersPhoto.com: 34, 42 (both), 64 (male), 66 (male, female), 78 (male dorsal), 82 (both), 94 (all), 104 (male dorsal), 118 (dorsal), 124 (dorsal), 172 (male ventral), 182 (female), 184 (all), 200 (male), 214 (male, female), 222 (male dorsal, female dorsal), 232 **Randy Emmitt:** 108 (both), 140 (all), 186, 198 (all) **Gary Meszaros/Dembinsky Photo Associates:** 170 (ventral), 190 (larva) **John and Gloria Tveten:** 66 (larva), 78 (male ventral), 80 (green larva, red larva), 86 (larvae), 90 (larva), 92, 102 (larva), 104 (male ventral, larva), 112 (all), 116 (larva), 132 (dorsal), 168 (larva), 170 (dorsal), 182 (male), 202 (larva), 204 (larva), 222 (ventral) **John and Gloria Tveten/KAC Productions:** 98, 126 **Elton Woodbury Collection/University of Florida:** 216 (both)
Jaret C. Daniels: all other photos

To the best of the publisher's knowledge, all photos were of live larvae and butterflies.

Book and Cover Design by Jonathan Norberg
Illustrations by Julie Martinez
Range Maps and Phenograms by Anthony Hertzel

10 9 8 7 6 5

Butterflies of Florida Field Guide
Copyright © 2003 by Jaret C. Daniels
Published by Adventure Publications
An imprint of AdventureKEEN
310 Garfield Street South
Cambridge, Minnesota 55008
(800) 678-7006
www.adventurepublications.net
All rights reserved
Printed in China

ISBN 978-1-59193-005-1 (pbk.)

TABLE OF CONTENTS
Introduction

WATCHING BUTTERFLIES IN FLORIDA

People are rapidly discovering the joy of butterfly gardening and watching. Both are simple, fun and rewarding ways to explore the natural world and bring the beauty of nature closer. Few other forms of wildlife are more attractive or as easily observed as butterflies. Butterflies occur just about everywhere. They can be found from suburban gardens and urban parks to rural meadows and remote natural areas. Regardless of where you may live, there are a variety of butterflies to be seen. *Butterflies of Florida Field Guide* is for those who wish to identify and learn more about common butterflies of Florida.

There are more than 725 species of butterflies found in North America north of Mexico. While the majority of these are regular breeding residents, others show up from time to time as rare tropical strays. In Florida, over 180 different butterflies have been recorded. Within that mix, some 40 are considered either unique to the state or occur mostly within its boundaries. Although such numbers pale in comparison to many tropical countries, the state boasts a rich and diverse butterfly fauna. To aid in your exploration of this remarkable group of insects, this field guide covers 102 of the most common and noteworthy species in Florida.

With a name like "The Sunshine State," Florida is destined to be a great place to observe and enjoy butterflies, but blue skies alone do not account for high species diversity. Much of Florida's abundant butterfly life is directly related to climate and geography. Totaling 58,560 square miles, this primarily long, narrow state represents the southernmost portion of the Southeast Coastal Plain. It has some 1,350 miles of coast and is literally surrounded on all but one side by warm marine waters. This helps to temper the severity of the seasons and provides a prolonged growing period. Additionally, Florida extends through a broad latitudinal gradient. The result is a significant variation in climate from warm temperate in the north to nearly tropical in the south.

It is this transition that makes Florida unique. The state essentially brings together two climatic regions. North

Florida and the Panhandle from Jacksonville to Ocala and west to Pensacola experience four distinct seasons. Here the winters are generally mild with occasional hard freezes and rare snowfall; the summers are hot and wet with temperatures regularly approaching 90°F, and the springs and falls are short but warm. This portion of Florida supports a diverse assemblage of temperate species, including many that you could also encounter in a New England deciduous forest or Midwestern prairie.

South Florida represents the other extreme. From just below Lake Okeechobee, things take a decidedly more tropical turn. In place of summer and winter, the seasons are best described as wet and dry. During the wet season, temperatures consistently peak in the 90s, the humidity is high and rain showers are regular and abundant. Conditions moderate somewhat in the dry season but rainfall totals drop dramatically. Luckily though, the thermometer rarely follows. The lack of freezing temperatures ensures a lush, year-round environment and helps to make South Florida a safe refuge for many tropical species.

Between these, in Central Florida, winters interrupt long periods of warm weather with cool nights and intermittent but brief periods of freezing temperatures. This unique peninsular highway, from Daytona Beach to the trailing edge of the Lake Wales Ridge south of Sebring, represents a transition zone where temperate and tropical species intersect. Here, there is a wonderfully rich array of butterflies.

In addition to climate, the proximity of Florida to the nearby islands of the West Indies makes it an exciting place to see butterflies. Over the course of time, many tropical species have found their way to South Florida and are now breeding residents. Others show up as occasional visitors or rare strays. Some have been blown in with hurricanes, dispersed naturally or even hitchhiked on plants or products.

WHAT ARE BUTTERFLIES?

Butterflies are insects. Along with moths, they comprise the Order Lepidoptera, a combination of Greek words meaning scale-winged, and can be differentiated from all other insects on that basis. Their four wings, as well as body, are typically almost entirely covered with numerous tiny scales. Overlapping like shingles on a roof, they make up the color and pattern of a butterfly's wings. Although generally wide and flat, some scales may be modified in shape, depending on the species and body location.

Butterflies and moths are closely related and often difficult to quickly tell apart. Nonetheless, there are some basic differences that are easy to identify even in the field. Generally, butterflies fly during the day, have large colorful wings that are held vertically together over the back when at rest, and bear distinctly clubbed antennae. In contrast, most moths are nocturnal. They are usually overall drabber in color and may often resemble dirty, hairy butterflies. At rest, they tend to hold their wings to the sides, and have feathery or threadlike antennae.

The following illustration points out the basic parts of a butterfly.

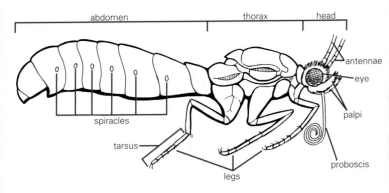

BUTTERFLY BASICS

Adult butterflies share several common characteristics, including six jointed legs, two compound eyes, two antennae, a hard exoskeleton and three main body segments: the head, thorax and abdomen.

Head

The head has two large compound eyes, two long clubbed antennae, a proboscis and two labial palpi. The rounded compound eyes are composed of hundreds of tiny individually lensed eyes. Together, they render a single, somewhat pixelated color image. Adult butterflies have good vision and are able to distinguish light in both the visible and ultraviolet range. Above the eyes are two long and slender antennae that are clubbed at the tip. They bear various sensory structures that help with orientation and smell. At the front of the head, below the eyes, are two protruding, hairy, brushlike structures called labial palpi. They serve to house and protect the proboscis, or tongue. The proboscis is a long flexible straw-like structure used for drinking fluids. It can be held tightly coiled below the head or extended when feeding. The length of a butterfly's proboscis determines the types of flowers and other foods from which it may feed.

Thorax

Directly behind the head is the thorax. It is an enlarged muscular portion of the body divided into three segments that bear six legs and four wings. The front pair of legs may be significantly smaller and modified in certain families. Each leg is jointed and contains five separate sections, the last of which is the tarsus (pl. tarsi) or foot, which bears a tiny, hooked claw at the end. In addition to enabling the butterfly to securely grasp leaves, branches or other objects, the tarsi have sensory structures that are used to taste. Adult females scratch a leaf surface with their front tarsi to release the leaf's chemicals and taste whether they have found the correct host plant. Above the legs are two pairs of wings. Made up of two thin membranes supported by rigid veins, the generally large, colorful wings are covered with millions of tiny scales that overlap like shingles on a roof. The wings are used for a variety of critical functions, including flight, thermoregulation, sex recognition, camouflage, mimicry and predator deflection.

Abdomen

The last section of a butterfly's body is the abdomen. This long, slender portion is comprised of ten segments and contains the reproductive, digestive and excretory systems along with a series of small lateral holes, called spiracles, for air exchange. The reproductive organs or genitalia are located at the end of the abdomen. Male butterflies have two modified structures called claspers that are used to grasp the female during copulation. Females possess a genital opening for mating and a second opening for egg laying. While these structures are often difficult to see in certain species, females generally have a much larger, "fatter-looking" abdomen because they carry a large complement of eggs.

THE BUTTERFLY LIFE CYCLE

All butterflies pass through a life cycle consisting of four developmental stages: egg, larva, pupa and adult. Regardless of adult size, they begin life as a small egg. A female butterfly may lay her eggs singly, in small clusters or in large groupings on or near the appropriate host plant. Once an egg hatches, the tiny larva begins feeding almost immediately. Butterfly larvae are herbivores—with the exception of Harvester larvae, which eat aphids—and they essentially live to eat. As a result, they can grow at an astonishing rate. Unlike humans, though, all insects including butterflies have an external skeleton. In order to grow, a developing caterpillar (or larva) must shed its skin, or molt, several times during its life. Each time the larva does, it discards its old, tight skin to make room for the new, roomier and often different-looking skin underneath. These different stages in a caterpillar's growth are called instars. Once fully grown, the larva stops eating and seeks a safe place to pupate. It usually attaches itself to a branch, twig or other surface with silk and molts for the last time to reveal the pupa (or chrysalis). Inside, the larval structures are broken down and reorganized into the form of an adult butterfly. At the appropriate time, the pupa splits open and a beautiful new butterfly emerges. The adult hangs quietly and begins to expand its crumpled wings by slowly forcing blood through the veins. After a few hours, its wings are fully hardened and the butterfly is ready to fly.

BUTTERFLY FAMILIES

Butterflies can be divided into five major families: Hesperiidae, Lycaenidae, Nymphalidae, Papilionidae and Pieridae. The members of each family have certain basic characteristics and behaviors that can be particularly useful for identification. Keep in mind that the features listed are only generalities, not hard and fast rules, and that there may be individual exceptions.

Hesperiidae: Skippers

Skippers are small- to medium-sized butterflies with robust, hairy bodies and relatively compact wings. They are generally brown, orange or white in color and their antennae bear short, distinct hooks at the tip. The adults have quick and erratic flight, usually low to the ground. Skippers can be divided into three main subfamilies: banded skippers (Subfamily Hesperiinae), giant-skippers (Subfamily Megathyminae) and spread-wing skippers (Subfamily Pyrginae).

Banded skippers (Subfamily Hesperiinae) are small orange or brown butterflies with somewhat pointed forewings. Many have dark markings or distinct black forewing stigmas. They readily visit flowers and hold their wings together over the back while feeding. Adults often perch or rest in a characteristic posture with forewings held partially open and hindwings separated and lowered further.

As their name suggests, *giant-skippers* (Subfamily Megathyminae) dwarf most other members of the family. They are medium-sized brown butterflies with yellow markings and thick, robust bodies. The adults have a fast and rapid flight. Males establish territories and generally perch on low vegetation. Adults do not visit flowers.

Spread-wing skippers (Subfamily Pyrginae) are generally dark, dull-colored butterflies with wide wings. Most have small, light spots on the forewings. Some species have hindwing tails. The adults often feed, rest and perch with their wings outstretched. They readily visit flowers.

Lycaenidae: Gossamer Wings

This diverse family includes harvesters, blues, hairstreaks and metalmarks. The adults are small and often brilliantly colored but easily overlooked. Within the family is Florida's smallest butterfly, the Eastern Pygmy-Blue. Throughout the state, blues and hairstreaks predominate, with harvesters and metalmarks represented by only one species each.

The **harvester** (Subfamily Miletinae) is the only North American member of this unique, primarily Old World, subfamily. It holds the distinction as our only butterfly with carnivorous larvae. Instead of feeding on plant leaves, the larvae devour woolly aphids. The adults do not visit flowers, but sip honeydew, a sugary secretion produced by their host aphids.

Aptly named, **blues** (Subfamily Polyommatinae) are generally bright blue in color on the wings above. The sexes differ and females may be brown or dark gray. The wings beneath are typically whitish-gray with dark markings and distinct hindwing eyespots. The eyes are wrapped around the base of the antennae. The palpi are reduced and close to the head. The adults have a moderately quick and erratic flight, usually low to the ground. At rest, they hold their wings together over the back. Males frequently puddle at damp ground. Most blues are fond of open, disturbed sites with weedy vegetation.

Metalmarks (Subfamily Riodininae) are characterized by metallic flecks of color or even overall merallic-looking wings. They have eyes entirely separate from the antennal bases, and the palpi are quite prominent. Metalmarks reach tremendous diversity in the tropics where they come in an almost unending array of colors and patterns. By contrast, most U.S. species are small rust, gray or brownish butterflies. They characteristically perch with their colorful wings outstretched and may often land on the underside of leaves, especially when disturbed. Adults have a low, scurrying flight. Several species are of conservation concern.

Hairstreaks (Subfamily Theclinae) tend to be larger in size than blues. The wings below are often intricately patterned and bear colorful eyespots adjacent to one or two small, distinct hair-like tails on each hindwing. The adults have a quick, erratic flight and can be a challenge to follow. They regularly visit flowers and hold their wings together over the back while feeding and at rest. Additionally, they have a unique behavior of moving their hindwings up and down when perched. The sexes regularly differ. Hairstreaks can be found in a wide range of habitats from dense woodlands to open, disturbed sites. Many species have a single spring generation.

Nymphalidae: Brush-Foots

Brush-foots are the largest and most diverse family of butterflies. Its members include emperors, leafwing butterflies, milkweed butterflies, longwing butterflies, true brush-foots and satyrs and wood nymphs. In all, the first pair of legs is significantly reduced and modified into small brush-like structures, giving the family its name and making it look as if they only have four legs.

Emperors (Subfamily Apaturinae) are medium-sized brownish butterflies with short, stubby bodies and a robust thorax. Their wings typically have dark markings and small dark eyespots. The adults are strong and rapid fliers. Males establish territories and perch on tree trunks or overhanging branches. At rest, they hold their wings together over the back. They feed on dung, carrion, rotting fruit or tree sap and do not visit flowers. Emperors inhabit rich woodlands and rarely venture far into open areas. They are nervous butterflies and difficult to closely approach.

Leafwings (Subfamily Charaxinae) are medium-sized butterflies with irregular wing margins. They are bright tawny orange above, but mottled gray to brown below and resemble a dead leaf when resting with their wings closed. The adults have a strong, rapid and erratic flight. They are nervous butterflies and difficult to closely approach. Males establish territories and perch on tree trunks or overhanging branches. Individuals also often land on the ground. They feed on dung, carrion, rotting fruit or tree sap and do not visit flowers.

Milkweed butterflies (Subfamily Danainae) are large butterflies with boldly marked black and orange wings. Their flight is strong and swift with periods of gliding. The adults are strongly attracted to flowers and feed with their wings folded tightly over the back. Males have noticeable black scent patches in the middle of each hindwing.

Longwing butterflies (Subfamily Heliconiinae) are colorful, medium- to large-sized butterflies with narrow, elongated wings, slender bodies, long antennae and large eyes. The flight varies from quick and erratic to slow and fluttering. The adults readily visit flowers and nectar with their wings outstretched. At rest, they hold their wings together over the back. Most individuals are long-lived.

True brush-foots (Subfamily Nymphalinae) are colorful, small- to medium-sized butterflies with no overall common wing shape. Most have stubby, compact bodies and a robust thorax. The adults have a strong, quick flight, usually low to the ground. Most are nervous and often difficult to approach. At rest, they hold their wings together over the back. Many are attracted to flowers while others feed on dung, carrion, rotting fruit or tree sap.

Satyrs and *wood nymphs* (Subfamily Satyrinae) are small- to medium-sized drab brown butterflies. Their wings are marked with dark stripes and prominent eyespots. The adults have a slow, somewhat bobbing flight usually low to the ground. They inhabit shady woodlands and adjacent open, grassy areas. The adults rarely visit flowers. They are instead attracted to dung, carrion, rotting fruit or tree sap. At rest, they hold their wings together over the back and are generally easy to closely approach. They regularly land on the ground.

Papilionidae: Swallowtails

Swallowtails are easily recognized by their large size and noticeably long hindwing tails. Within Florida, only the

Polydamus Swallowtail lacks tails. They are generally dark in color with bold markings. The adults have a swift and powerful flight, usually several meters off the ground, and regularly visit flowers. Most swallowtails continuously flutter their wings while feeding. Males often puddle at damp ground. They generally are found in and along woodland areas and adjacent open sites.

Pieridae: Sulphurs and Whites

Members of the family are small- to medium-sized butterflies. As their name suggests, the adults are typically some shade of white or yellow. Many have dark markings. Most species are sexually dimorphic and seasonally variable. The adults have a moderately quick and erratic flight, usually low to the ground. They are fond of flowers and hold their wings together over the back while feeding. Males often puddle at damp ground. **Sulphurs** (Subfamily Coliadinae) and **whites** (Subfamily Pierinae) are common butterflies of open, disturbed sites where their weedy larval host plants abound.

OBSERVING BUTTERFLIES IN THE FIELD

While butterflies are entertaining and beautiful to watch, correctly identifying them can often be a challenge. But it's generally not as difficult as it might seem. With a little practice and some basic guidelines, you can quickly learn to peg that unknown butterfly.

One of the first and most obvious things to note when you spot a butterfly is its size. You will discover that butterflies generally come in one of three basic dimensions: small, medium and large. This system may sound ridiculously arbitrary at first, but when you begin to regularly observe several different butterflies together in the field, these categories quickly start to make sense. For a starting point, follow this simple strategy: the next time you see a Monarch butterfly, pay close attention to its size. You may wish to use your hand as a reference. Most Monarchs have a wingspan close to the length of your palm (about four inches) as measured from the base of your fingers to the start of your wrist. This is considered a large butterfly. From here it's basically a matter of fractions. A medium-sized butterfly by comparison would have a wingspan of generally about half that size (about two inches). Finally, a butterfly would be considered small if it had a wingspan one quarter that of a Monarch (around one inch).

Next, pay close attention to color and pattern of the wings. This field guide is organized by color, and you can quickly navigate to the appropriate section. First, start by noting the overall ground color. Is it, for example, primarily black, yellow, orange or white? Then try to identify any major pattern elements. Does the butterfly have any distinct stripes, bands or spots? Depending on the behavior of the butterfly in the wild, keep in mind that the most visible portion of a butterfly may either be the upper surface of the wings (dorsal surface) or the underside of the wings (ventral surface). If you have a particularly cooperative subject, you may be able to closely observe both sides. Finally, carefully note the color and position of any major markings. For example, if the butterfly has a wide yellow band on the forewing, is it positioned in the middle of the wing or along the outer edge? Lepidopterists have a detailed vocabulary for wing pattern positions. The following illustrations of general wing features and wing areas should help you become familiar with some terminology.

Next, note the shape of the butterfly's wings, particularly the forewings. Are they generally long and narrow, rounded, broad, pointed or angled? Butterflies such as the Gulf Fritillary and Zebra Longwing have noticeably elongated wings. Others, like the Carolina Satyr and Eastern Tailed-Blue, have short, generally rounded wings. Next, do the wings have any unique features? Many swallowtails and hairstreaks, for instance, have distinct hindwing tails, while Question Marks and Ruddy Daggerwings have visibly irregular wing margins. Clues like this can help you quickly narrow the butterfly down to a particular family or distinguish it from a similarly colored species.

The way a butterfly flies may also be useful for identification. While it is generally difficult to easily pick up particular features or color patterns when a butterfly is moving, its flight pattern can often be very distinctive. Carefully follow the butterfly as it flies and watch how it behaves in the air.

Wing Features

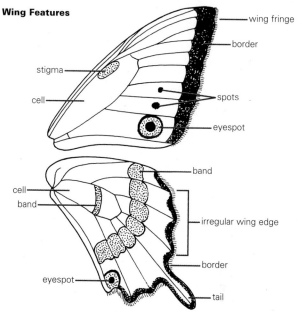

Wing Areas

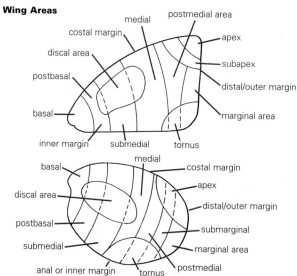

Is it soaring above your head or scurrying rapidly along the ground? Is it moving fast and erratically, or fluttering slowly about? Monarchs, for instance, have a very unique flight pattern. They flap their wings quickly several times, glide for bit, and then quickly flap their wings again. Other butterflies, such as most wood nymphs and satyrs, have a characteristic low, bobbing flight.

Sometimes you can gain important clues about a butterfly by the way it behaves when feeding. Next time you see a butterfly feeding, watch its wings. Does it hold them tightly closed, spread them wide open, or move them in a fluttering motion? Most swallowtails, for example, continuously flutter their wings. This behavior is a quick and reliable diagnostic that can be seen from a fair distance.

Note the habitat in which the butterfly occurs. Is it darting between branches along a shady and moist woodland path? Perched on the top of a grass blade in a saltwater marsh? Bobbing among low grasses in a wet prairie? Fluttering from one flower to the next in a fallow agricultural field? Many butterflies have strong habitat preferences. Some are restricted to a single particular habitat while others may occur in a wide range of habitats.

Sometimes even the date can offer a useful hint. Many hairstreaks, for instance, are univoltine, meaning they produce just one generation. As a result, the adults occur only during a narrow window of time each spring. Similarly, several butterflies overwinter as adults. They may be active at times when few other species are around.

Butterfly observation and identification are skills, and it takes time and practice to master them. To speed up the learning curve, you may also wish to join a local butterfly gardening or watching club or society. The members can help give advice, accompany you in the field, or share directions to great butterfly watching spots.

BUTTERFLY GARDENING

One of the easiest ways to observe local butterflies is to plant a butterfly garden. Even a small area can attract a great variety of species directly to your yard. For best results, include both adult nectar sources and larval host plants. Most adult butterflies are generalists and will visit a broad range of colorful flowers in search of nectar. Developing larvae, on the other hand, typically have very discriminating tastes and often rely on only a few very specific plant species for food. For assistance with starting a butterfly garden, seek the guidance of local nursery professionals. They can help you determine which plants will grow well in your area. This field guide provides a list of larval host plants for each species, as well as a listing of good nectar plants. These lists begin on page 250.

BUTTERFLY Q & A:

What's the difference between a butterfly and a moth?

While there is no one simple answer to this question, butterflies and moths generally differ based on their overall habits and structure. Butterflies are typically active during the day (diurnal), while moths predominantly fly at night (nocturnal). Butterflies possess slender antennae that are clubbed at the end. Those of moths vary from long narrow filaments to broad fern-like structures. At rest, butterflies tend to hold their wings together vertically over the back. Moths rest with their wings extended flat out to the sides or folded alongside the body. Butterflies generally have long, smooth and slender bodies. The bodies of moths are often robust and hairy. Finally, most butterflies are typically brightly colored, while most moths tend to be dark and somewhat drab.

What can butterflies see?

Butterflies are believed to have very good vision and to see a single color image. Compared to humans, they have an expanded range of sensitivity and are able to distinguish wavelengths of light into the ultraviolet range.

Do butterflies look the same year-round?

Many butterflies produce distinct seasonal forms that differ markedly in color, size, reproductive activity and behavior. Good examples within Florida include the Common Buckeye, Barred Sulphur and Sleepy Orange.

The seasonal forms are determined based on a variety of environmental cues (temperature, rainfall, day length) that immature stages experience during development. Warm summer temperatures and long days forecast conditions that are highly favorable for continued development and reproduction. Summer-form individuals are generally lighter in color, short-lived, and reproductively active. As fall approaches, cooler temperatures and shortening day lengths mean future conditions may be unfavorable for continued development and reproduction. Winter-form adults are generally darker, display increased pattern elements, larger in size, longer lived, and survive the winter months in a state of reproductive diapause.

Do caterpillars have eyes?

Yes, caterpillars or larvae generally have six pairs of simple eyes called ocelli. They are able to distinguish basic changes in light intensity but are believed to be incapable of forming an image.

How do caterpillars defend themselves?

Caterpillars or larvae are generally plump, slow moving creatures that represent an inviting meal for many predators. To protect themselves, caterpillars employ a variety of different strategies. Many, like the Zebra Longwing or Pipevine Swallowtail, sequester specific chemicals from their host plants that render them highly distasteful or toxic. These caterpillars are generally brightly colored to advertise their unpalatability. Others rely on deception or camouflage to avoid being eaten. Palamedes Swallowtail larvae have large, conspicuous false eyes on an enlarged thorax that help them resemble a small snake or lizard. By contrast, larvae of the Georgia Satyr are solid green and extremely well camouflaged against the green leaves of their host. Some larvae conceal their whereabouts by constructing shelters. American Painted Lady larvae weave leaves and flowerheads together with silk and rest safely inside when not actively feeding. Still others have formidable spines and hairs or produce irritating or foul-smelling chemicals to deter persistent predators.

Do butterfly caterpillars make silk?

Yes, butterfly larvae produce silk. While they don't typically spin an elaborate cocoon around their pupa like moths, they use silk for a variety of purposes, including the construction of shelters, anchoring or attaching their chrysalids, and to gain secure footing on leaves and branches.

What happens when a butterfly's scales rub off?

Contrary to the old wives' tale, if you touch a butterfly's wing and remove scales in the process it is still capable of flying. In fact, a butterfly typically continuously loses scales during its life from normal wing wear. Scales serve a variety of purposes, from thermoregulation and camouflage to pheromone dispersal and species or sex recognition, but are not critical for flight. Once gone, however, the scales are permanently lost and will not grow back.

Why do butterflies gather at mud puddles?

Adult butterflies are often attracted to damp or moist ground and may congregate at such areas in large numbers. In most cases, these groupings, or "puddle clubs," are made up entirely of males. They drink from the moisture to gain water and salts (sodium ions) that happen to come into solution. This behavior helps males replenish the sodium ions lost when they pass a packet of sperm and accessory gland secretions to the female during copulation. The transferred nutrients have been shown to play a significant role in egg production and, thus, female reproductive output.

How long do butterflies live?

In general, most butterflies are extremely short-lived and survive in the wild for an average of about two weeks. There are, of course, numerous exceptions to this rule. Florida's state butterfly, the Zebra Longwing, is a perfect example. Adults of this butterfly may survive for 4–6 months. Still others, particularly species that migrate long distances and/or overwinter as adults, are capable of surviving for extended periods of time.

Where do butterflies go at night?
Where do they go during a rainstorm?

In the evening or during periods of inclement weather, most butterflies seek shelter under the leaves of growing plants or among vegetation.

Do all butterflies visit flowers?

All butterflies are fluid feeders. While a large percentage of them rely on sugar-rich nectar as the primary energy source for flight, reproduction and general maintenance, many species also feed on, or exclusively utilize, the liquids and dissolved nutrients produced by other food resources such as dung, carrion, rotting fruit or vegetation, sap and bird droppings.

Do butterflies grow?

No. An adult butterfly is fully grown upon emergence from its chrysalis.

How do caterpillars grow?

A caterpillar's job in life is to eat and grow. But larvae, like all other insects, have an external skeleton. Therefore, in order to increase in size, they must shed their skin, or molt, several times during development. Essentially, their skin is like a trash bag. It is packed full of food until there is no more room. Once full, it is discarded for a larger, baggier one underneath and the process continues.

What eats butterflies?

Butterflies face an uphill battle for survival. Out of every one hundred eggs produced by a female butterfly, approximately only one percent survive to become an adult. And as an adult, the odds don't get much better. Various birds, small mammals, lizards, frogs, toads, spiders and other insects all prey on butterflies.

What's the difference between a chrysalis and a cocoon?

Once fully grown, both moth and butterfly caterpillars molt a final time to form a pupa. Most moths surround their pupae with a constructed silken case called a cocoon. By contrast, a butterfly pupa, frequently termed a chrysalis, is generally naked. In most cases, butterfly chrysalids are attached to a leaf, twig or other surface with silk. In some instances, they may be unattached or surrounded by a loose silken cocoon.

Are all butterfly scales the same?

No. The scales on a butterfly's wings and body come in a variety of different sizes and shapes. Some may be extremely elongated and resemble hairs while others are highly modified for the release of pheromones during courtship. Those responsible for making up wing color and pattern are generally wide and flat. They are attached at the base and overlap like shingles on a roof. The colors we see are the result of either pigments contained in the scales or the diffraction of light caused by scale structure. Iridescent colors such as blue, green, purple and silver usually result from scale structure. While pigmented scales are the norm, many species have a combination of both types on their wings.

BUTTERFLY QUICK-COMPARE

Common Sootywing
pg. 35

Great Purple Hairstreak
pg. 37

Atala
pg. 39

Red Admiral
pg. 41
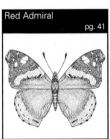

Mangrove Skipper
pg. 43

Zebra Longwing
pg. 45

Red-spotted Purple
pg. 47
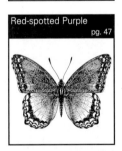

Zebra Swallowtail
pg. 49

Black Swallowtail
pg. 51

Pipevine Swallowtail
pg. 53

Spicebush Swallowtail
pg. 55

Polydamus Swallowtail
pg. 57

Palamedes Swallowtail
pg. 59

Eastern Tiger Swallowtail
pg. 61

Cassius Blue
pg. 63

Ceraunus Blue
pg. 65

Eastern Tailed-Blue
pg. 67

Miami Blue
pg. 69

Summer Azure
pg. 71

White M Hairstreak
pg. 73

Great Purple Hairstreak
pg. 75

Eastern Pygmy-Blue
pg. 77

Tawny-edged Skipper
pg. 79

Henry's Elfin
pg. 81

Eufala Skipper pg. 83	Whirlabout pg. 85	Banded Hairstreak pg. 87
	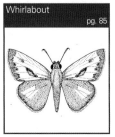	
Striped Hairstreak pg. 89	Southern Hairstreak pg. 91	Salt Marsh Skipper pg. 93
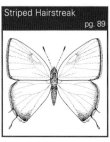	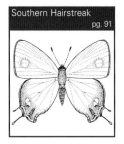	
Sachem pg. 95	Southern Broken-Dash pg. 97	Little Glassywing pg. 99

Carolina Satyr pg. 101	Clouded Skipper pg. 103	Dun Skipper pg. 105
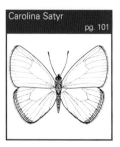		

Twin-spot Skipper pg. 107	Southern Cloudywing pg. 109	Northern Cloudywing pg. 111
	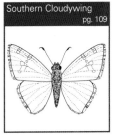	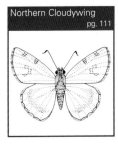
Juvenal's Duskywing pg. 113	Gemmed Satyr pg. 115	Horace's Duskywing pg. 117

Hoary Edge pg. 119	Georgia Satyr pg. 121	Viola's Wood Satyr pg. 123
	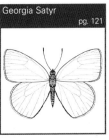	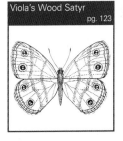
Dorantes Skipper pg. 125	Ocola Skipper pg. 127	Long-tailed Skipper pg. 129
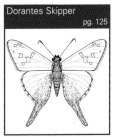		

American Snout
pg. 131

Brazilian Skipper
pg. 133

Southern Pearly Eye
pg. 135

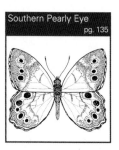

Silver-spotted Skipper
pg. 137

Common Buckeye
pg. 139

Zabulon Skipper
pg. 141

Hackberry Butterfly
pg. 143

Common Wood Nymph
pg. 145

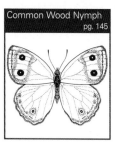

Tawny Emperor
pg. 147

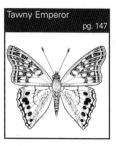

Mangrove Buckeye
pg. 149

Yucca Giant-Skipper
pg. 151

Schaus' Swallowtail
pg. 153

Giant Swallowtail pg. 155	Red-banded Hairstreak pg. 157	Bartram's Hairstreak pg. 159
		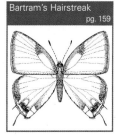

Gray Hairstreak pg. 161	Sweadner's Hairstreak pg. 163	Malachite pg. 165

Southern Skipperling pg. 167	Little Metalmark pg. 169	Least Skipper pg. 171

Pearl Crescent pg. 173	Phaon Crescent pg. 175	Fiery Skipper pg. 177

Whirlabout
pg. 179

Harvester
pg. 181

Delaware Skipper
pg. 183

Sachem
pg. 185

Palatka Skipper
pg. 187

Sleepy Orange
pg. 189

Orange Sulphur
pg. 191

Variegated Fritillary
pg. 193

Painted Lady
pg. 195

American Painted Lady
pg. 197

Zabulon Skipper
pg. 199

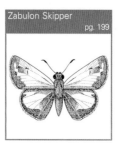

Large Orange Sulphur
pg. 201

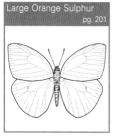

30

Question Mark pg. 203	Goatweed Butterfly pg. 205	Gulf Fritillary pg. 207
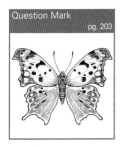		

Viceroy pg. 209	Florida Leafwing pg. 211	Queen pg. 213
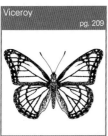		

Julia pg. 215	Ruddy Daggerwing pg. 217	Monarch pg. 219

Common/White Checkered-Skipper pg. 221	Tropical Checkered-Skipper pg. 223	Barred Sulphur pg. 225

Checkered White
pg. 227

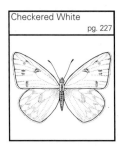

Cabbage White
pg. 229

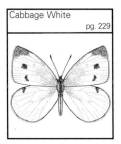

Great Southern White
pg. 231

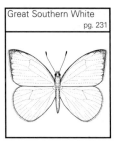

Florida White
pg. 233

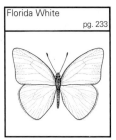

White Peacock
pg. 235

Dainty Sulphur
pg. 237

Little Sulphur
pg. 239

Barred Sulphur
pg. 241

Southern Dogface
pg. 243

Cloudless Sulphur
pg. 245

Orange-barred Sulphur
pg. 247

Eastern Tiger Swallowtail
pg. 249

Common Name
Scientific Name

color section indicators →

Family/Subfamily: tells which family and subfamily the butterfly belongs to (see p. 11–15 for descriptions)

Wingspan: gives minimum and maximum wing spans, from one forewing tip to the other

Above: description of upper, or dorsal, surface of wings

Below: description of lower, or ventral, surface of wings

Sexes: describes differences in appearance between male and female

Egg: description of eggs and where they are deposited

Larva: description of the butterfly's larva, or caterpillar

Larval Host Plants: lists plants that eggs and larva are likely to be found on

Habitat: describes where you're likely to find the butterflies

Broods: lists number of broods, or generations, hatched in a span of one year

Abundance: when the butterflies are flying, this tells you how often you're likely to encounter them

Compare: describes differences among similar-looking species

range map shows where in Florida this butterfly is present

phenogram: shows population flux throughout the year

Resident: predictably present
Stray: rarely to occasionally present

Resident Stray ►

Jan. Feb. Mar. Apr. May June July Aug. Sept. Oct. Nov. Dec.

Dorsal (above)

Ventral (below)

silhouette behind Comments section shows actual average size of butterfly

illustration shows field marks and features to look for

Comments: The Common Sootywing indeed looks as if it fell into a pail of ashes. It is avidly drawn to available flowers. Adults have a low, erratic flight and scurry around quickly, stopping occasionally to rest on nearby vegetation or bare soil with their wings spread. The larvae construct individual shelters on the host by folding over part of a leaf with silk.

Common Sootywing
Pholisora catullus

Family/Subfamily: Skippers (Hesperiidae)/
Spread-wing Skippers (Pyrginae)

Wingspan: 0.90–1.25" (2.3–3.2 cm)

Above: shiny dark brown to black with a variable number
of small white forewing spots and a few on top of the
head

Below: as above but paler brown

Sexes: similar, although female often has larger white
forewing spots

Egg: reddish pink, laid singly on upperside of host leaves

Larva: pale gray-green with a narrow dorsal stripe, pale
green lateral stripes, a black collar and black head;
body is covered with numerous tiny yellow-white dots,
each bearing a single hair

Larval Host Plants: Lamb's Quarters, Mexican Tea,
Spiny Amaranth

Habitat: open, disturbed sites including roadsides, old
fields, utility easements and fallow agricultural land

Broods: multiple generations

Abundance: occasional to common

Compare: Northern Cloudywing (pg. 111), Southern
Cloudywing (pg. 109) and Horace's Duskywing (pg.
117) have glassy, semitransparent forewing spots.

Resident

Jan. Feb. Mar. Apr. May June July Aug. Sept. Oct. Nov. Dec.

male

Dorsal (above)
small white spots
otherwise black

white spots on head

occasionally has a row
of small white spots
on hindwing

Ventral (below)

35

Female

Larva

Comments: The Great Purple Hairstreak is impressive in size compared to most members of its family. It typically dwells high up in the canopy close to its mistletoe host. Nonetheless, adults readily come down to feed on available flowers and can be closely observed. Easily identified by its orange abdomen, the butterfly's bold ventral coloration warns predators that it is highly distasteful.

Great Purple Hairstreak
Atlides halesus

Family/Subfamily: Gossamer Wings (Lycaenidae)/ Hairstreaks (Theclinae)

Wingspan: 1.0–1.7" (2.5–4.3 cm)

Above: male is bright metallic purple-blue with black margins and two hindwing tails; female is dull black with metallic blue scaling limited to wing bases

Below: dull brownish black with metallic green and blue spots near tail and red spots at wing bases; underside of abdomen reddish orange; head and thorax have white spots

Sexes: dissimilar; female duller with less blue

Egg: green, laid singly on host leaves

Larva: green with numerous short hairs

Larval Host Plants: Mistletoe

Habitat: woodland edges and adjacent open areas

Broods: multiple generations

Abundance: occasional

Compare: White M Hairstreak (pg. 73) is smaller with a narrow white M on the underside of the hindwing near the tails; small white spot along leading edge of the hindwing below.

Resident

Jan. Feb. Mar. Apr. May June July Aug. Sept. Oct. Nov. Dec.

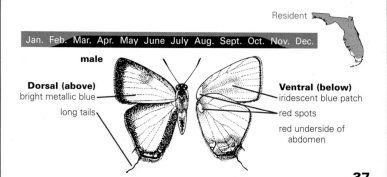

male

Dorsal (above)
bright metallic blue

long tails

Ventral (below)
iridescent blue patch

red spots

red underside of abdomen

37

Male

Larva

Comments: The boldly colored Atala lacks the hindwing tails characteristic of most hairstreaks. Once abundant throughout southern portions of mainland Florida, commercial harvesting of the butterfly's host plant for starch during the late 1800s severely reduced population numbers. Continued urbanization and the resulting loss of critical costal habitat pushed the species even closer to extinction. By 1965, the Atala had been reduced to a single known colony. However, persistent efforts by conservationists, combined with the rapid growth in popularity of cycads for landscape use, helped the butterfly make a remarkable recovery.

Atala
Eumaeus atala

Family/Subfamily: Gossamer Wings (Lycaenidae)/ Hairstreaks (Theclinae)

Wingspan: 1.6–1.9" (4.1–4.8 cm)

Above: male is velvety black with metallic green on forewing, basal area of hindwing and along hindwing margin; female is black with metallic blue on forewing and along hindwing margin; abdomen bright reddish orange; lacks tail

Below: black with numerous small metallic blue spots on hindwing and bright reddish orange patch near abdomen

Sexes: similar, although female has metallic blue scaling along costal margin of forewing

Egg: white, laid in clusters on new growth of host

Larva: bright red with yellow spots along the back

Larval Host Plants: Coontie

Habitat: hammocks and adjacent areas with host

Broods: multiple generations

Abundance: occasional; very localized

Compare: unique

Resident

Jan. Feb. Mar. Apr. May June July Aug. Sept. Oct. Nov. Dec.

male

Dorsal (above)
iridescent green
red abdomen
iridescent green spots
no tail

Ventral (below)
black wings
large red spot
small iridescent blue spots

39

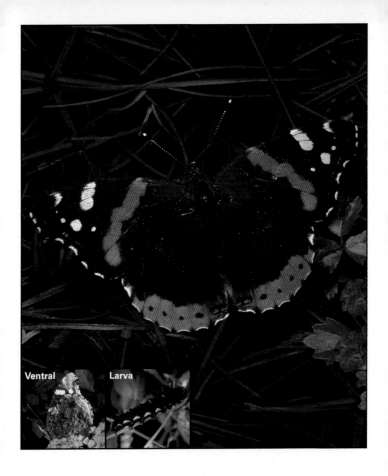

Ventral

Larva

Comments: The Red Admiral is a medium-sized dark butterfly that is quickly distinguished from any other species by its distinctive red forewing band. Particularly common in spring, the butterfly will readily explore suburban gardens. Adults have a quick, erratic flight. Males frequently perch on low vegetation or on the ground in sunlit locations. The larvae construct individual shelters on the host by folding together one or more leaves with silk.

Red Admiral
Vanessa atalanta

Family/Subfamily: Brush-foots (Nymphalidae)/
True Brush-foots (Nymphalinae)

Wingspan: 1.75–2.50" (4.4–6.4 cm)

Above: dark brownish black with red hindwing border
and distinct, red median forewing band; forewing has
small white spots near apex

Below: forewing as above with blue scaling and paler
markings; hindwing mottled with dark brown, blue and
cream in bark-like pattern

Sexes: similar

Egg: small green eggs laid singly on host leaves

Larva: variable; pinkish gray to charcoal with lateral row
of cream crescent-shaped spots and numerous
branched spines

Larval Host Plants: False Nettle, Pellitory and nettles

Habitat: moist woodlands, forest edges, roadside ditches, along canals and ponds, wetlands and gardens

Broods: multiple generations; adults overwinter

Abundance: occasional; locally abundant

Compare: unique

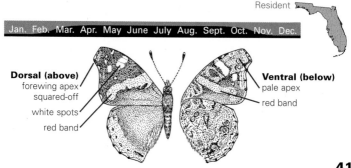

Resident

Jan. Feb. Mar. Apr. May June July Aug. Sept. Oct. Nov. Dec.

Dorsal (above)
forewing apex
squared-off

white spots

red band

Ventral (below)
pale apex

red band

Larva

Comments: Impressive in size and color, the Mangrove Skipper is arguably one of the most attractive skippers in Florida. Adults have a fast, powerful flight but regularly stop to nectar at available flowers. When feeding, they sit with their wings spread and are easily observed. They frequently perch on the underside of leaves. The brightly colored larvae construct individual shelters on the host by folding over sections of a leaf with silk. Adults can be found throughout the year.

Mangrove Skipper
Phocides pigmalion

Family/Subfamily: Skippers (Hesperiidae)/ Spread-wing Skippers (Pyrginae)

Wingspan: 2.0–2.5" (5.1–6.4 cm)

Above: brownish black with iridescent blue scaling; hind-wing tapers into a small, stubby tail and has a submarginal row of faint light blue spots

Below: forewing dull brownish black; hindwing black with blue sheen and several faint pale blue bands; head has white face

Sexes: similar

Egg: laid singly on host leaves

Larva: crimson with yellow bands and two yellow patches on head capsule; larval color changes to cream-white in last instar

Larval Host Plants: Red Mangrove

Habitat: coastal mangroves

Broods: multiple generations

Abundance: occasional to common

Compare: unique

Resident

Jan. Feb. Mar. Apr. May June July Aug. Sept. Oct. Nov. Dec.

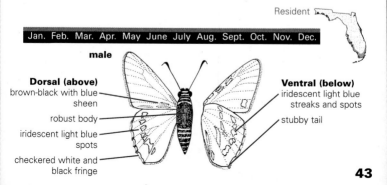

male

Dorsal (above)
brown-black with blue sheen

robust body

iridescent light blue spots

checkered white and black fringe

Ventral (below)
iridescent light blue streaks and spots

stubby tail

Ventral

Larva

Comments: The Zebra Longwing is the state butterfly of Florida. Aptly named, it is quickly identified by the yellow-white stripes and extremely elongated wings. It rarely spends long periods of time in open, sunny locations but is an abundant visitor to shadier gardens and yards. Adults have slow, graceful flight, and adeptly maneuver through dense vegetation. A member of a primarily tropical genus, it cannot endure prolonged exposure to freezing temperatures. Adults are extremely long-lived and may survive for several months.

Zebra Longwing
Heliconius charitonius

Family/Subfamily: Brush-foots (Nymphalidae)/
Longwing Butterflies (Heliconiinae)

Wingspan: 2.9–3.5" (7.4–8.9 cm)

Above: elongated black wings with pale yellow stripes

Below: as above with small red basal spots

Sexes: similar

Egg: yellow, laid in small groups on new growth and tendrils of host

Larva: white with small black spots and numerous long
black spines

Larval Host Plants: Various Passion-Flowers including
Maypop, Corky-Stemmed Passion-Flower and Yellow
Passion-Flower

Habitat: gardens, woodlands, hammocks, forest edges
and adjacent open, disturbed areas

Broods: multiple generations

Abundance: common

Compare: unique

Resident Stray

Jan. Feb. Mar. Apr. May June July Aug. Sept. Oct. Nov. Dec.

Dorsal (above)
black with yellow
stripes
long antennae
long abdomen

Ventral (below)
elongated wings
small red spots on
wing base

Ventral

Larva

Comments: The Red-Spotted Purple, although lacking a
hindwing tail, mimics the toxic Pipevine Swallowtail to
gain protection from would-be predators. It is a common butterfly of immature woodlands but is rarely
encountered in large numbers. Adults have a strong,
gliding flight and are often quite wary. Males perch on
sunlit branches along trails or forest borders and make
periodic exploratory flights. Adults occasionally visit
flowers but often prefer rotting fruit, dung, carrion or
tree sap.

Red-Spotted Purple
Limenitis arthemis astyanax

Family/Subfamily: Brush-foots (Nymphalidae)/ Admirals and Relatives (Limenitidinae)

Wingspan: 3.0–3.5" (7.6–8.9 cm)

Above: dark bluish black with iridescent blue scaling on hindwing and small orange and white spots near forewing apex

Below: brownish black; hindwings have a row of red-orange spots toward the outer margin and at wing base; forewing has orange cell bars

Sexes: similar

Egg: gray-green, laid singly on the tips of host leaves

Larva: mottled green, brown and cream with two long, knobby horns on thorax

Larval Host Plants: Wild Cherry

Habitat: open woodlands, forest edges and adjacent open areas

Broods: multiple generations

Abundance: occasional

Compare: Pipevine Swallowtail (pg. 53) has hindwing tail and a low, rapid flight; continually flutters wings when nectaring.

Resident

Jan. Feb. Mar. Apr. May June July Aug. Sept. Oct. Nov. Dec.

Dorsal (above)
iridescent blue

hindwing is squared off

Ventral (below)
pale forewing apex

red-orange spots

Larva

Comments: The black and white striped Zebra Swallowtail can be confused with no other butterfly in the state. Adults have a low, rapid flight and adeptly maneuver among understory vegetation. Males regularly patrol territories for females. This swallowtail has a proportionately short proboscis and is thus unable to nectar at many long, tubular flowers. It instead prefers composites and is regularly attracted to white flowers. Summer-form individuals are larger, darker, and have longer hindwing tails.

Zebra Swallowtail
Eurytides marcellus

Family/Subfamily: Swallowtails (Papilionidae)/ Swallowtails (Papilioninae)

Wingspan: 2.5–4.0" (6.4–10.2 cm)

Above: white with black stripes and long, slender tails; hindwings bear a bright red patch above the eyespot; spring-forms are smaller, lighter and have shorter tails

Below: as above, but with a red stripe through hindwing

Sexes: similar

Egg: light green, laid singly on host leaves or budding branches

Larva: several color forms; may be green, green with light blue and yellow stripes or charcoal with white and yellow stripes

Larval Host Plants: various pawpaws

Habitat: woodlands, pinelands, pastures, forest edges and old fields

Broods: multiple generations

Abundance: occasional to common

Compare: unique

Resident

Jan. Feb. Mar. Apr. May June July Aug. Sept. Oct. Nov. Dec.

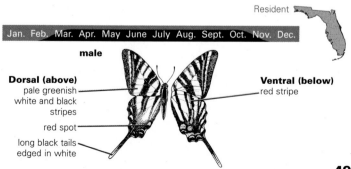

male

Dorsal (above)
pale greenish white and black stripes

red spot

long black tails edged in white

Ventral (below)
red stripe

Male

Female

Larva

Comments: The Black Swallowtail is one of our most commonly encountered garden butterflies. Its plump, green larvae, often referred to as parsley worms, feed on many cultivated herbs and may occasionally become minor nuisance pests. It is equally at home along farm roads or in rural meadows as suburban yards and urban parks. Males have a strong, rapid flight and frequently perch on low vegetation. Both sexes are exceedingly fond of flowers and readily stop to nectar. It is one of six eastern butterflies that mimic the toxic Pipevine Swallowtail to gain protection from predators.

Black Swallowtail
Papilio polyxenes

Family/Subfamily: Swallowtails (Papilionidae)/ Swallowtails (Papilioninae)

Wingspan: 2.5–4.2" (6.4–10.7 cm)

Above: male is black with a broad, postmedian yellow band and a row of marginal yellow spots; female is mostly black with increased blue hindwing scaling and marginal yellow spots, the yellow postmedian band is reduced; both sexes have a red hindwing eyespot with a central black pupil, and a yellow-spotted abdomen

Below: hindwing has orange-tinted yellow spot bands

Sexes: dissimilar; female has reduced yellow postmedian band and increased blue hindwing scaling above

Egg: yellow, laid singly on host leaves

Larva: green with black bands and yellow-orange spots

Larval Host Plants: wild and cultivated members of the Carrot Family including dill, fennel and parsley

Habitat: old fields, roadsides, pastures, disturbed sites, suburban gardens, agricultural land

Broods: multiple generations, late February to November

Abundance: occasional

Compare: Spicebush Swallowtail (pg. 55) is larger, has green-blue spots and lacks black-centered hindwing eyespot. Pipevine Swallowtail (pg. 53) is mostly black and lacks yellow marking.

Resident

Jan. Feb. Mar. Apr. May June July Aug. Sept. Oct. Nov. Dec.

male

Dorsal (above)
yellow bands
blue scaling
black "pupil" in center of spot
tail

Ventral (below)
yellow-orange bands
faint yellow-orange cell spot

Male

Larva

Comments: A relatively small member of the family, the Pipevine Swallowtail nevertheless has a strong, rapid flight. Adults frequently visit flowers but rarely linger at any one blossom for long. They continuously flutter their wings while feeding. The velvety black larvae sequester various toxins from their host. These chemicals render the larvae and adults highly distasteful to many predators. As a result, several other butterfly species mimic the color pattern of the Pipevine Swallowtail in order to gain protection.

Pipevine Swallowtail
Battus philenor

Family/Subfamily: Swallowtails (Papilionidae)/
Swallowtails (Papilioninae)

Wingspan: 2.75–4.00" (7.0–10.2 cm)

Above: an overall black butterfly; male has iridescent
greenish blue hindwings; female is duller black with a
single row of white spots near the wing margins

Below: hindwings below are iridescent blue with a row
of prominent orange spots

Sexes: dissimilar; female is dull black with a more prominent row of white spots

Egg: brownish orange, laid singly or in small clusters

Larva: velvety black with orange spots and numerous
long, fleshy tubercles

Larval Host Plants: various pipevine species, especially Virginia Snakeroot

Habitat: fields, pastures, roadsides, pinelands, woodlands

Broods: multiple generations

Abundance: occasional

Compare: Spicebush Swallowtail (pg. 55) is larger with
prominent pale greenish blue crescent-shaped spots
along the wing margins. Red-Spotted Purple (pg. 47)
lacks hindwing tails. Black Swallowtail (pg. 51) has yellow bands and an orange eyespot with a black center
on the hindwing.

Resident

Jan.	Feb.	Mar.	Apr.	May	June	July	Aug.	Sept.	Oct.	Nov.	Dec.

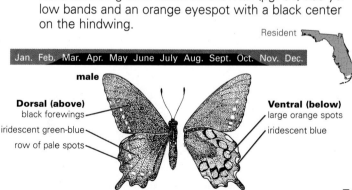

male

Dorsal (above)
black forewings
iridescent green-blue
row of pale spots

Ventral (below)
large orange spots
iridescent blue

53

Male

Larva

Comments: The Spicebush Swallowtail is one of four
Florida butterflies that mimic the unpalatable Pipevine
Swallowtail to gain protection from predators. Adults
are strong, agile fliers but rarely stray far from their
preferred woodland habitat and are infrequent in urban
locations. A true lover of flowers, they readily venture
out into nearby open areas in search of nectar and
continuously flutter their wings while feeding. The larvae make individual shelters by curling up both edges
of a leaf with silk. They rest motionless inside when
not actively feeding. At maturity, the larvae turn yellow
and wander in search of an appropriate site to pupate.

Spicebush Swallowtail
Papilio troilus

Family/Subfamily: Swallowtails (Papilionidae)/ Swallowtails (Papilioninae)

Wingspan: 3.5–5.0" (8.9–12.7 cm)

Above: black with a row of large, pale greenish blue spots along the margin; hindwings have greenish blue scaling, a single, orange eyespot and a large orange spot along the leading margin

Below: black with postmedian band of blue scaling bordered by row of yellow-orange spots on each side; abdomen black with longitudinal rows of light spots

Sexes: similar, female has duller hindwing scaling

Egg: cream, laid singly on the underside of host leaves

Larva: green above, reddish below with enlarged thorax, two false eyespots and several longitudinal rows of blue spots

Larval Host Plants: Sassafras, Camphor-tree, Red Bay and Spicebush

Habitat: woodlands, forest edges, wooded swamps, pastures, old fields and suburban gardens

Broods: multiple generations

Abundance: occasional

Compare: Pipevine Swallowtail (pg. 53) lacks submarginal greenish blue spots.

Resident

| Jan. | Feb. | Mar. | Apr. | May | June | July | Aug. | Sept. | Oct. | Nov. | Dec. |

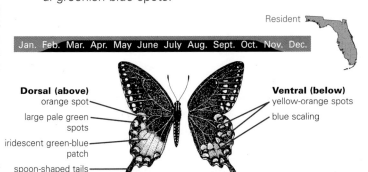

Dorsal (above)
orange spot
large pale green spots
iridescent green-blue patch
spoon-shaped tails

Ventral (below)
yellow-orange spots
blue scaling

55

Larva

Comments: The Polydamus Swallowtail lacks the characteristic hindwing tails common to most other North American members of the family. This trait, combined with its broad, yellow wing bands, makes the species easy to identify. It is a fast and powerful flier with a preference for open areas. Primarily a tropical butterfly, it is rarely found north of the Florida border. It is a common butterfly of suburban and urban gardens. Adults are good colonizers and readily disperse long distances in search of suitable hosts.

Polydamus Swallowtail
Battus polydamus

Family/Subfamily: Swallowtails (Papilionidae)/ Swallowtails (Papilioninae)

Wingspan: 4.0–5.0" (10.2–12.7 cm)

Above: black with a prominent yellow band along the outer margin of wings; lacks tails

Below: hindwings have marginal row of narrow red spots; thorax and abdomen black with red spots

Sexes: similar

Egg: amber-brown, laid in small clusters on new growth of the host

Larva: robust, chocolate-brown with numerous short orange, fleshy tubercles

Larval Host Plants: various native and ornamental pipevine species

Habitat: fields, gardens, woodland edges, suburban parks, disturbed sites

Broods: multiple generations

Abundance: occasional to locally common

Compare: Black Swallowtail (pg. 51) is smaller with yellow spot bands above and hindwing tails.

Resident

Jan. Feb. Mar. Apr. May June July Aug. Sept. Oct. Nov. Dec.

Dorsal (above)
black wings
yellow band
no tails

Ventral (below)
red spots
scalloped margin

Larva

Comments: The Palamedes is Florida's most commonly encountered swallowtail. Adults have a strong, directed flight and avidly nectar at available blooms. Males often congregate at moist ground to imbibe diluted minerals and salts. The larvae have an enlarged thorax with a prominent pair of false eyespots that resemble the head of a small lizard or snake.

Palamedes Swallowtail
Papilio palamedes

Family/Subfamily: Swallowtails (Papilionidae)/ Swallowtails (Papilioninae)

Wingspan: 3.5–5.5" (8.9–14.0 cm)

Above: black with a broad, postmedian yellow band and a row of marginal yellow spots

Below: hindwing has a band of blue scaling bordered by median and submarginal rows of yellow-orange spots; narrow yellow line near wing base runs parallel to the abdomen, no other black colored swallowtail in Florida has this marking

Sexes: similar

Egg: cream, laid singly on host leaves; new growth preferred

Larva: green above, reddish below with enlarged thorax and two false eyespots

Larval Host Plants: Red Bay, Swamp Bay, Silk Bay

Habitat: wooded swamps, hammocks, forest edges, suburban gardens, moist woodlands and evergreen swamps

Broods: multiple generations

Abundance: occasional to abundant

Compare: Black Swallowtail (pg. 51) is smaller and has yellow abdominal spots and a black-centered hindwing eyespot.

Resident

Jan. Feb. Mar. Apr. May June July Aug. Sept. Oct. Nov. Dec.

Dorsal (above)
yellow band
yellow tail edged in black

Ventral (below)
narrow yellow stripe
orange crescents

Dark-form female

Female Male pg. 249 Larva

Comments: Easily recognized by its bold, black stripes and yellow wings, the Tiger Swallowtail is one of the state's most familiar butterflies. Adults have a strong, agile flight and often soar high in the treetops. A common and conspicuous garden visitor, adults are readily drawn to available flowers. Males often congregate in large numbers at mud puddles or moist ground. Dark-form females mimic the toxic Pipevine Swallowtail to gain protection from predators. Females exhibit numerous intermediate-colored forms.

Eastern Tiger Swallowtail
Papilio glaucus

Family/Subfamily: Swallowtails (Papilionidae)/ Swallowtails (Papilioninae)

Wingspan: 3.5–5.5" (8.9–14.0 cm)

Above: yellow with black forewing stripes and broad black wing margins; single row of yellow spots along outer edge of each wing

Below: yellow with black stripes and black wing margins; hindwing margins have increased blue scaling and a single submarginal row of yellow-orange, crescent-shaped spots; abdomen yellow with black stripes

Sexes: dissimilar; male always yellow but females have two color forms; yellow female has increased blue scaling in black hindwing border; dark-form female is mostly black with extensive blue hindwing markings

Egg: green, laid singly on upper surface of host leaves

Larva: green; enlarged thorax and two small false eyespots

Larval Host Plants: Wild Cherry, White Ash and Sweet Bay

Habitat: mixed forests, wooded swamps, hammocks, forest edges, suburban gardens

Broods: multiple generations

Abundance: occasional to common

Compare: Yellow-form unique. Pipevine Swallowtail (pg. 53) is much smaller.

Resident

Jan. Feb. Mar. Apr. May June July Aug. Sept. Oct. Nov. Dec.

male

Dorsal (above)
black stripes
wide black border
yellow spots

Ventral (below)
yellow-orange spots
blue scaling

Male

Larva

Comments: The Cassius Blue is abundant throughout south Florida but occasionally disperses northward beyond the state's border. Many of these isolated records, however, may be the result of immature stages of the butterfly "piggybacking" on shipments of the popular landscape plant, Plumbago, to various commercial nurseries.

Cassius Blue
Leptotes cassius

Family/Subfamily: Gossamer Wings (Lycaenidae)/ Blues (Polyommatinae)

Wingspan: 0.75–1.0" (1.9–2.5 cm)

Above: blue with thin black border and white wing fringe; female is light blue with broad gray borders; hindwing bears two dark marginal spots

Below: whitish with numerous gray bands and spots; hindwing has two orange-rimmed black and metallic blue eyespots

Sexes: dissimilar; female has duller, more heavily patterned blue-white wings

Egg: greenish blue, laid singly on flower buds, flowers or immature fruit of host

Larva: variable; green to green with pinkish red markings

Larval Host Plants: numerous plants including Wild Tamarind, Leadwort, Wild Plumbago, Blackbead and milk peas

Habitat: open, disturbed sites including roadsides, vacant or weedy fields, coastal dunes, forest edges and gardens

Broods: multiple generations

Abundance: occasional to abundant

Compare: Ceraunus Blue (pg. 65) is darker gray beneath with white-rimmed black spots near wing base.

Resident Stray

Jan. Feb. Mar. Apr. May June July Aug. Sept. Oct. Nov. Dec.

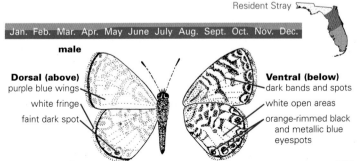

male

Dorsal (above)
purple blue wings
white fringe
faint dark spot

Ventral (below)
dark bands and spots
white open areas
orange-rimmed black and metallic blue eyespots

Male

Ventral

Comments: The Ceraunus Blue is one of the most commonly encountered blues in Florida. It scurries erratically among low-growing vegetation and may be easily overlooked. Adults often rest with their wings partially open, providing a good view of their attractive dorsal coloration. Both sexes actively visit flowers. Males periodically congregate at damp ground.

Ceraunus Blue
Hemiargus ceraunus

Family/Subfamily: Gossamer Wings (Lycaenidae)/ Blues (Polyommatinae)

Wingspan: 0.75–1.00" (1.9–2.5 cm)

Above: male is bright lavender blue with a narrow black border and white wing fringe; single black dot along hindwing margin

Below: light gray with numerous dark markings and spots; hindwing has a prominent orange-rimmed black spot with metallic blue scaling

Sexes: dissimilar; female is brown with blue scaling at wing bases

Egg: greenish blue, laid singly on flower buds of host

Larva: highly variable; green with a red lateral stripe to highly patterned pinkish red

Larval Host Plants: numerous Fabaceous plants including Hairy Indigo, Creeping Indigo, Partridge Pea and milk peas

Habitat: open, disturbed sites including roadsides, vacant fields, utility easements and fallow agricultural land

Broods: multiple generations

Abundance: occasional to common

Compare: Cassius Blue (pg. 63) is generally larger, and is chalky white beneath with numerous dark bands.

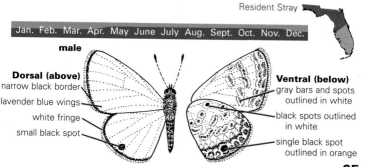

Resident Stray

Jan. Feb. Mar. Apr. May June July Aug. Sept. Oct. Nov. Dec.

male

Dorsal (above)
narrow black border
lavender blue wings
white fringe
small black spot

Ventral (below)
gray bars and spots outlined in white
black spots outlined in white
single black spot outlined in orange

65

Male

Female   Ventral   Larva

Comments: The Eastern Tailed-Blue, although generally abundant throughout most of the eastern United States, is infrequently encountered in Florida. It is typically relegated to the northernmost portions of the state. Adults have a weak, dancing flight and readily stop to nectar. Males often gather in small clusters on damp ground. Do not rely solely on the presence of hindwing tails for identification, as they are fragile and may often be broken off.

Eastern Tailed-Blue
Everes comyntas

Family/Subfamily: Gossamer Wings (Lycaenidae)/ Blues (Polyommatinae)

Wingspan: 0.75–1.00" (1.9–2.5 cm)

Above: male is blue with brown border; female is brownish gray; both sexes have one or two small orange and black hindwing spots above single tail

Below: silvery-gray with numerous dark spots and bands; hindwing has two small orange-capped black spots above tail

Sexes: similar, although female has reduced blue above

Egg: pale green, laid singly on flowers or young leaves of host

Larva: variable, typically green with dark dorsal stripe and light lateral stripes

Larval Host Plants: various herbaceous Fabaceae including clovers, bush clovers and beggarweeds

Habitat: open, disturbed sites including roadsides, vacant lots and old fields

Broods: multiple generations

Abundance: uncommon to occasional

Compare: Summer Azure (pg. 71) lacks hindwing tails. Gray Hairstreak (pg. 161) has distinct black-and-white (occasionally orange) ventral hindwing stripe.

Resident

Jan. Feb. Mar. Apr. May June July Aug. Sept. Oct. Nov. Dec.

male

Dorsal (above)
bright blue

one or two orange-capped black spots

tail

Ventral (below)
black spots and bars outlined in white

one or two orange-capped black spots

Female

Larva

Comments: The Miami Blue is endemic to Florida. Primarily a coastal species, once abundant and wide-spread throughout the southern portion of the state, the species' overall distribution and numerical abundance has been significantly reduced over the last few decades. Ever-expanding urbanization and the associated loss of coastal habitat have all but eliminated the Miami Blue from the south Florida mainland. In recent years, this alarming trend of decline has continued in the Keys. Now, the butterfly only occurs in small, isolated colony sites. It is currently listed as endangered by the state of Florida.

Miami Blue
Hemiargus thomasi

Family/Subfamily: Gossamer Wings (Lycaenidae)/ Blues (Polyommatinae)

Wingspan: 0.75–1.10" (1.9–2.8 cm)

Above: male is bright blue with narrow black wing border and white fringe; hindwing has single, small black dot along margin; female is bright blue with broad dark borders; distinct orange-capped black spot on hindwing

Below: gray with wide white postmedian band; hindwing has four black basal spots and orange-capped black spot

Sexes: similar, although female has reduced blue scaling above and orange hindwing spot

Egg: whitish, laid singly on flower buds, new growth and developing seed pods of host

Larva: variable; green to maroon with dark head and light lateral stripe

Larval Host Plants: Balloon Vine and nickerbean

Habitat: tropical hardwood hammock margins, scrub and pine rocklands and adjacent open areas

Broods: multiple generations

Abundance: rare; very localized; endangered

Compare: Ceraunus Blue (pg. 65) is smaller, with incomplete white postmedian band on ventral hindwing. Cassius Blue (pg. 63) is white beneath with prominent dark bands.

Resident

Jan. Feb. Mar. Apr. May June July Aug. Sept. Oct. Nov. Dec.

female

Dorsal (above)
wide dark margin

orange-capped
black spot

Ventral (below)
four black basal spots

wide white band

two black spots, one
orange-capped

Larva

Comments: Although the Summer Azure ranges throughout much of the Eastern U.S., it is an uncommon butterfly in Florida, being relegated primarily to the northern portion of the state. Adults of this small dusty blue butterfly are found in and along woodlands but readily venture out into nearby open areas in search of nectar. They have a moderately slow dancing flight and are often encountered fluttering high among the branches of trees and shrubs. Males often congregate at damp ground.

Summer Azure
Celastrina neglecta

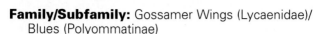

Family/Subfamily: Gossamer Wings (Lycaenidae)/ Blues (Polyommatinae)

Wingspan: 0.80–1.25" (2.0–3.2 cm)

Above: male is light blue with narrow, faint dark forewing border; female is light blue with increased white scaling and wide, dark forewing border

Below: chalky white with small dark spots and bands

Sexes: dissimilar, female has increased white scaling above and wide forewing borders

Egg: whitish green, laid singly on flower buds of host

Larva: variable; green to pinkish green with dark dorsal stripe and cream bands

Larval Host Plants: flowers of various trees and shrubs including New Jersey Tea, dogwoods and sumac

Habitat: open, deciduous woodlands, forest edges, road-sides, old fields and utility easements and gardens

Broods: multiple generations

Abundance: rare to occasional

Compare: Spring Azure (*Celastrina ladon*) is more heavily marked below. Cassius Blue (pg. 63) and Ceraunus Blue (pg. 65) have orange and black ventral hindwing eyespot. Eastern Tailed-Blue (pg. 67) has small tail and ventral orange hindwing spots.

Resident

Jan. Feb. Mar. Apr. May June July Aug. Sept. Oct. Nov. Dec.

male

Dorsal (above)
solid blue with some white scaling on hindwing

Ventral (below)
chalky white
faint dark spots

Female

Comments: The White M Hairstreak is named for the narrow white band on the underside of the hindwing that forms the letter M. The true beauty of this diminutive species can be seen mainly during flight, when the bright iridescent blue scaling of the upper wing surfaces flashes in the sunlight. Adults readily explore open areas adjacent to their habitat for available flowers. Adults have a quick, erratic flight and can be difficult to follow.

White M Hairstreak
Parrhasius m-album

Family/Subfamily: Gossamer Wings (Lycaenidae)/ Hairstreaks (Theclinae)

Wingspan: 0.9–1.3" (2.3–3.3 cm)

Above: male is bright iridescent blue with broad, black margins and two hindwing tails; female is dull black with blue scaling limited to wing bases

Below: brownish gray; hindwing has a single red eyespot above tail, white spot along leading margin, and a narrow white line forming a distinct M in middle of wing

Sexes: dissimilar; female duller with less blue

Egg: whitish, laid singly on twigs or buds of host

Larva: variable, dark green to mauve

Larval Host Plants: various oaks including Live Oak

Habitat: forest edges, oak hammocks, pine-oak scrub and adjacent open areas

Broods: multiple generations

Abundance: occasional to common

Compare: Great Purple Hairstreak (pg. 75) is larger and lacks white M and red spot on ventral hindwing. Southern Hairstreak (pg. 91) has longer tails and a more extensive orange submarginal band.

Resident

Jan. Feb. Mar. Apr. May June July Aug. Sept. Oct. Nov. Dec.

male

Dorsal (above)
iridescent blue
wide black borders

Ventral (below)
white spot
white M
red spot
blue patch

73

Male

Larva

Comments: The Great Purple Hairstreak is impressive in size compared to most members of its family. It typically dwells high up in the canopy close to its mistletoe host. Nonetheless, adults readily come down to feed on available flowers and can be closely observed. Easily identified by its orange abdomen, the butterfly's bold ventral coloration warns predators that it is highly distasteful.

Great Purple Hairstreak
Atlides halesus

Family/Subfamily: Gossamer Wings (Lycaenidae)/
Hairstreaks (Theclinae)

Wingspan: 1.0–1.7" (2.5–4.3 cm)

Above: male is bright metallic purple-blue with black
margins and two hindwing tails; female is dull black
with metallic blue scaling limited to wing bases

Below: dull brownish black with metallic green and blue
spots near tail and red spots at wing bases; underside
of abdomen reddish orange; head and thorax have
white spots

Sexes: dissimilar; female duller with less blue

Egg: green, laid singly on host leaves

Larva: green with numerous short hairs

Larval Host Plants: Mistletoe

Habitat: woodland edges and adjacent open areas

Broods: multiple generations

Abundance: occasional

Compare: White M Hairstreak (pg. 73) is smaller with a
narrow white M on the underside of the hindwing near
the tails; small white spot along leading edge of the
hindwing below.

Resident

| Jan. | Feb. | Mar. | Apr. | May | June | July | Aug. | Sept. | Oct. | Nov. | Dec. |

male

Dorsal (above)
black patch
bright metallic blue
long tails

Ventral (below)
iridescent blue patch
red spots
red underside of
abdomen

Larva

Comments: Appropriately named, the Eastern Pygmy-
Blue is the smallest butterfly in Florida. Adults have a
low, weak flight and scuttle just above the surface of
their host plants. Nonetheless, their diminutive size
often makes individuals a challenge to follow when on
the wing. Easily identified, it is the only blue in the
state with a row of four silvery-black spots on the
hindwings below. Although abundant in certain locations, individual colonies are often sporadic and highly
localized.

Eastern Pygmy-Blue
Brephidium isophthalma

Family/Subfamily: Gossamer Wings (Lycaenidae)/
Blues (Polyommatinae)

Wingspan: 0.50–0.75" (1.3–1.9 cm)

Above: brown with row of dark spots along the outer
margin of the hindwing

Below: brown with numerous white streaks and bands;
hindwing margin has row of black spots with silver
highlights

Sexes: similar

Egg: greenish blue, laid singly on all parts of host

Larva: green with dark head

Larval Host Plants: glassworts

Habitat: salt marshes and adjacent coastal areas

Broods: multiple generations

Abundance: occasional; locally abundant

Compare: Ceraunus Blue (pg. 65) is larger, gray beneath
with single black hindwing eyespot. Cassius Blue (pg.
63) is larger, strongly banded beneath with two black
hindwing eyespots.

Resident

Jan. Feb. Mar. Apr. May June July Aug. Sept. Oct. Nov. Dec.

Dorsal (above)
brown fringe
row of small black
spots

Ventral (below)
brown fringe
four prominent black
spots

77

Male

Male

Comments: The Tawny-edged Skipper's distinct orange band along the upper edge of the forewing is visible from both the dorsal and ventral surfaces. This highly visible feature quickly differentiates it from many other common brown skippers. The species may be frequently encountered in more suburban locations including home gardens. Adults have a low, rapid flight and often alight on bare soil or low vegetation.

Tawny-edged Skipper
Polites themistocles

Family/Subfamily: Skippers (Hesperiidae)/ Banded Skippers (Hesperiinae)

Wingspan: 0.8–1.2" (2.0–3.0 cm)

Above: male is dark brown with prominent black stigma and tawny orange scaling along forewing costa; female is dark brown with small yellow spots across forewing and reduced orange along costal margins

Below: light brown to olive brown with distinct contrasting orange scaling along costal margin of forewing

Sexes: dissimilar; female darker with reduced orange coloration

Egg: greenish white, laid singly on host leaves

Larva: reddish brown with dark dorsal stripe and black head

Larval Host Plants: various grasses including panic grasses

Habitat: stream corridors, wet meadows and fields

Broods: two generations

Abundance: occasional

Compare: Baracoa Skipper (*Polites baracoa*) is smaller, has more rounded wings, and a band of light spots across the hindwing below.

Resident

Jan. Feb. Mar. Apr. May June July Aug. Sept. Oct. Nov. Dec.

male

Dorsal (above)
orange
sinuous black stigma

Ventral (below)
orange scaling
brassy colored without spots

79

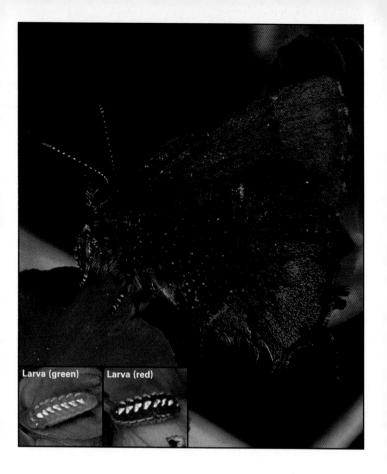

Larva (green)

Larva (red)

Comments: Henry's Elfin is a small butterfly delicately marked on the wings below with brown and violet. Unlike most hairstreaks, elfins lack, or have reduced, stubby hindwing tails. Found in variety of semi-open areas, this spring species rarely strays far from stands of its larval host. Males regularly perch high on branches and await passing females. Adults have a fast, erratic flight but regularly stop to visit the blossoms of various flowering trees.

Henry's Elfin
Callophrys henrici

Family/Subfamily: Gossamer Wings (Lycaenidae)/ Hairstreaks (Theclinae)

Wingspan: 0.9–1.2" (2.3–3.0 cm)

Above: brown with amber red along hindwing margin; hindwing has short, stubby tail

Below: brown; hindwing distinctly two-toned with dark brown basal half and light brown outer half; gray frosting along outer margin

Sexes: similar

Egg: whitish, laid singly on host twigs or flower buds

Larva: variable; green to reddish with oblique white markings

Larval Host Plants: Redbud, Dahoon Holly, American Holly and Yaupon Holly

Habitat: deciduous woodlands, forest edges, roadsides, old fields and utility easements where hosts occur

Broods: single spring generation

Abundance: occasional; local

Compare: Eastern Pine Elfin (*Callophrys niphon*) has strongly banded ventral hindwing.

Resident

Jan. Feb. Mar. Apr. May June July Aug. Sept. Oct. Nov. Dec.

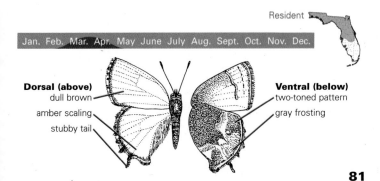

Dorsal (above)
dull brown
amber scaling
stubby tail

Ventral (below)
two-toned pattern
gray frosting

81

Larva

Comments: The Eufala Skipper is a year-round resident of the warm Gulf Coast and Florida. It is unable to survive prolonged exposure to freezing temperatures. Adults avidly visit available flowers and frequent home gardens. They have a rapid, erratic flight but pause regularly to perch or nectar and are easily observed. The underside of the wings are pale gray brown and often appear faded.

Eufala Skipper
Lerodea eufala

Family/Subfamily: Skippers (Hesperiidae)/
Banded Skippers (Hesperiinae)

Wingspan: 0.90–1.25" (2.3–3.2 cm)

Above: grayish brown with several tiny white spots on forewing; subapical spots form small, straight band

Below: light brown to tan, often with faint, light hindwing spots

Sexes: similar

Egg: cream, laid singly on or near host leaves

Larva: green with green and yellow stripes; head is brownish orange below and cream above

Larval Host Plants: various grasses, including Bermuda Grass

Habitat: open, grassy areas including old fields, roadsides, vacant lots, pineland edges and clearings, and utility easements

Broods: multiple generations

Abundance: occasional

Compare: The Three-spotted Skipper (*Cymaenes tripunctatus*) is warm brown below with distinct light hindwing spots.

Resident

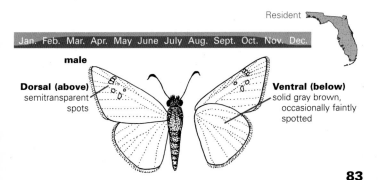

Jan. Feb. Mar. Apr. May June July Aug. Sept. Oct. Nov. Dec.

male

Dorsal (above)
semitransparent spots

Ventral (below)
solid gray brown, occasionally faintly spotted

83

Female

Male pg. 179

Comments: The Whirlabout is a diminutive skipper with two distinct rows of squarish spots on the hindwings below. This species is sexually dimorphic. Males are tawny orange and considerably brighter than their drab brown female counterparts. It regularly expands its range each summer, establishing temporary breeding colonies throughout the southeast from Maryland to Texas. Living up to its name, adults have a low, erratic flight and scurry quickly around, periodically stopping to perch or nectar. Avidly fond of flowers, the butterfly is a frequent garden visitor.

Whirlabout
Polites vibex

Family/Subfamily: Skippers (Hesperiidae)/
Banded Skippers (Hesperiinae)

Wingspan: 1.00–1.25" (2.5–3.2 cm)

Above: elongated wings; golden orange with black borders and black stigma; female is dark brown with cream spots on forewing

Below: hindwing yellow in male or bronze brown in female with two loose bands of large dark brown spots

Sexes: dissimilar; female brown above with little orange scaling; olive brown below with similar pattern as male

Egg: white, laid singly on host leaves

Larva: brownish green with thin, dark dorsal stripe and black head

Larval Host Plants: various grasses including Bermuda Grass, St. Augustine Grass and Crabgrass

Habitat: open, disturbed areas including old fields, roadsides, vacant lots, open woodlands, forest edges, parks, lawns and gardens

Broods: multiple generations

Abundance: common to abundant

Compare: Fiery Skipper (pg. 177) is similar in size and color but has scattered, tiny dark spots on ventral hindwing.

Resident

Jan. Feb. Mar. Apr. May June July Aug. Sept. Oct. Nov. Dec.

male

Dorsal (above)
golden orange
large black stigma
jagged black border

Ventral (below)
large dark brown spots
golden yellow

85

Larvae

Comments: A small, inconspicuous butterfly, the Banded Hairstreak is closely associated with mixed hardwood forests and can frequently be found along woodland edges or in sunlit clearings. Adults frequently visit flowers and are particularly fond of white sweet clover. Males perch on shrubs or low, overhanging limbs and aggressively defend established territories by engaging passing intruders.

Banded Hairstreak
Satyrium calanus

Family/Subfamily: Gossamer Wings (Lycaenidae)/
Hairstreaks (Theclinae)

Wingspan: 1.00–1.25" (2.5–3.2 cm)

Above: unmarked dark brown with two hindwing tails

Below: brown to slate gray; hindwing has dark postmedian band outlined on outer side with white and a red-capped black spot and blue patch near tails

Sexes: similar

Egg: pinkish brown, laid singly on twigs of host

Larva: variable, green to grayish brown with a light lateral stripe

Larval Host Plants: various oaks and hickories

Habitat: forest edges and adjacent open areas

Broods: single generation

Abundance: occasional

Compare: Striped Hairstreak (pg. 89) has wider, more extensive bands beneath and an orange-capped blue patch near tail.

Resident

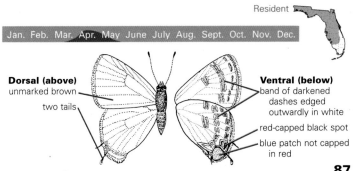

Jan. Feb. Mar. Apr. May June July Aug. Sept. Oct. Nov. Dec.

Dorsal (above)
unmarked brown

two tails

Ventral (below)
band of darkened dashes edged outwardly in white

red-capped black spot

blue patch not capped in red

87

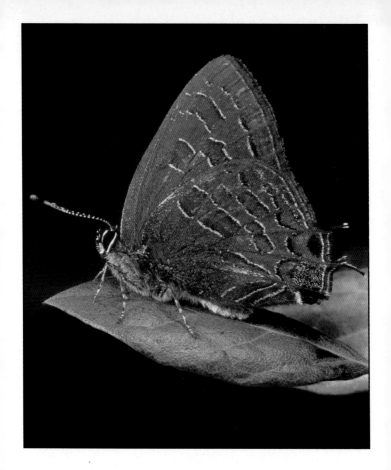

Comments: The Striped Hairstreak is typically encountered with a variety of other spring hairstreak species at available flowers along woodland margins. Although widespread, it is seldom abundant and typically observed as single individuals. Females lay the small, flattened eggs singly on host twigs. The eggs overwinter and the young larvae hatch the following spring and feed on the buds and young leaves.

Striped Hairstreak
Satyrium liparops

Family/Subfamily: Gossamer Wings (Lycaenidae)/ Hairstreaks (Theclinae)

Wingspan: 1.0–1.3" (2.5–3.3 cm)

Above: unmarked dark brown with two hindwing tails

Below: brown to slate gray with numerous wide, dark bands outlined in white; hindwing has blue patch and several red-capped black spots near tails

Sexes: similar

Egg: pinkish brown, flattened, laid singly on twigs of host

Larva: bright green with yellow-green oblique stripes and dark dorsal line

Larval Host Plants: various trees and shrubs including hawthorn, Black Cherry and Sparkleberry

Habitat: forest clearings, woodland edges and adjacent open areas with secondary growth

Broods: single spring generation

Abundance: occasional

Compare: Banded Hairstreak (pg. 87) has less extensive, narrower ventral bands and lacks the reddish-orange cap on the blue hindwing patch.

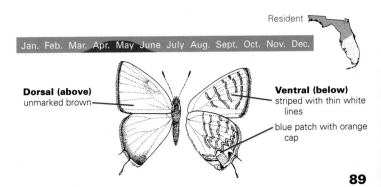

Resident

Jan. Feb. Mar. Apr. May June July Aug. Sept. Oct. Nov. Dec.

Dorsal (above)
unmarked brown

Ventral (below)
striped with thin white lines

blue patch with orange cap

Larva

Comments: The Southern Hairstreak has a quick, erratic flight and can be difficult to follow. Both sexes avidly visit flowers and are particularly fond of white composites. Although producing only a single generation, the butterfly has a prolonged flight period that may extend over many weeks. Females deposit the small eggs on host twigs near the buds. They overwinter on the tree until the following spring when the young larvae hatch and feed on the bounty of new growth.

Southern Hairstreak
Fixsenia favonius

Family/Subfamily: Gossamer Wings (Lycaenidae)/ Hairstreaks (Theclinae)

Wingspan: 1.0–1.3" (2.5–3.3 cm)

Above: dark brown with faint orange scaling

Below: brown; hindwing has jagged black-and-white line, white spot along leading margin, and distinct, broad reddish orange submarginal band tapering toward forewing; large blue patch and several black dots near long tails

Sexes: similar

Egg: pinkish brown, laid singly on twigs of host; eggs overwinter

Larva: green with yellow lateral stripes and dark green dorsal line

Larval Host Plants: various oaks

Habitat: woodland edges, oak scrub and adjacent open areas

Broods: single spring generation

Abundance: occasional to common

Compare: White M Hairstreak (pg. 73) has single red ventral hindwing spot.

Resident

Jan. Feb. Mar. Apr. May June July Aug. Sept. Oct. Nov. Dec.

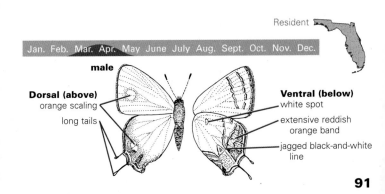

male

Dorsal (above)
orange scaling
long tails

Ventral (below)
white spot
extensive reddish orange band
jagged black-and-white line

Comments: The Salt Marsh Skipper's light wing veins and distinct white dash on the hindwing quickly separate it from all other similar-looking skippers. Adults have a low, rapid flight and frequently visit available flowers along nearby roads or in adjacent fields. Little detailed information is known about the biology of the immature stages.

Salt Marsh Skipper
Panoquina panoquin

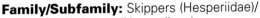

Family/Subfamily: Skippers (Hesperiidae)/
Banded Skippers (Hesperiinae)

Wingspan: 1.1–1.3" (2.8–3.3 cm)

Above: brown with small light spots across forewing

Below: light brown with light veins and distinct cream
dash in center of hindwing

Sexes: similar

Egg: light green, laid singly on host leaves

Larva: yellow green

Larval Host Plants: Salt Grass

Habitat: salt marshes and adjacent open areas, roadsides

Broods: multiple generations

Abundance: occasional; locally common

Compare: Brazilian Skipper (pg. 133) and Ocola Skipper
(pg. 127) lack pale ventral wing venation and distinct
cream dash in center of hindwing.

Resident

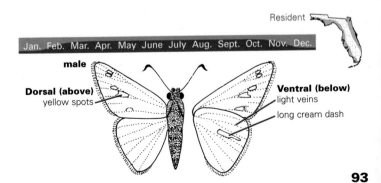

Jan. Feb. Mar. Apr. May June July Aug. Sept. Oct. Nov. Dec.

male

Dorsal (above)
yellow spots

Ventral (below)
light veins

long cream dash

Female

Male pg. 185 **Female** **Male**

Comments: The Sachem shares its affinity for open, disturbed sites with the Whirlabout and Fiery Skipper with which it often flies. Adults have a quick, darting flight that is usually low to the ground. All three species are somewhat nervous butterflies, but readily congregate at available flowers. Together, they often form a circus of activity with several pausing briefly to perch or nectar before one flies up and disturbs the others, only to alight again moments later.

Sachem
Atalopedes campestris

Family/Subfamily: Skippers (Hesperiidae)/ Banded Skippers (Hesperiinae)

Wingspan: 1.0–1.5" (2.5–3.8 cm)

Above: elongated wings; male is golden orange with brown borders and large, black stigma; female is dark brown with golden markings in wing centers; forewing has black median spot and several semitransparent spots

Below: variable; hindwing golden brown in male, brown in female with pale postmedian patch or band of spots

Sexes: dissimilar; female darker with reduced orange markings

Egg: white, laid singly on host leaves

Larva: greenish brown with thin, dark dorsal stripe and black head

Larval Host Plants: various grasses including Bermuda Grass and Crabgrass

Habitat: open, disturbed areas including old fields, pastures, roadsides, parks, lawns and gardens

Broods: multiple generations

Abundance: common to abundant

Compare: Fiery Skipper (pg. 177) and Whirlabout (pg. 85) have dark spots on the ventral hindwing.

Resident

Jan. Feb. Mar. Apr. May June July Aug. Sept. Oct. Nov. Dec.

male

Dorsal (above)
large squarish stigma
golden orange

Ventral (below)
large pale patch or postmedian band

Comments: The Southern Broken-Dash's unusual name comes from the noticeable separation of the forewing stigma that resembles two disconnected black lines. It is a frequent garden visitor. Fond of flowers, the adults sit quietly on available blossoms and are easy to close-ly observe or photograph. Superficially similar to, and formerly considered the same species as the more widespread Northern Broken-Dash, it has more red-dish orange coloration below.

Southern Broken-Dash
Wallengrenia otho

Family/Subfamily: Skippers (Hesperiidae)/
Banded Skippers (Hesperiinae)

Wingspan: 1.0–1.5" (2.5–3.8 cm)

Above: male is dark brown with brownish orange along
costal margin and in center of hindwing; forewing has
broken black stigma near elongated orange spot;
female is dark brown with several small cream-orange
spots across forewing

Below: hindwing reddish brown with faint band of light
spots

Sexes: dissimilar; female darker with reduced orange
markings and pale forewing spots

Egg: pale green, laid singly on host leaves

Larva: light green with dark mottling and dark head

Larval Host Plants: various grasses including St.
Augustine Grass and Crabgrass

Habitat: moist woodlands, forest edges, wetlands, roadsides, pastures, old fields and gardens

Broods: multiple generations

Abundance: common to abundant

Compare: Sachem (pg. 95) has more elongated wings
and broad pale ventral hindwing patch. Northern
Broken-Dash (*Wallengrenia egeremet*) is duller brown
below.

Resident

Jan. Feb. Mar. Apr. May June July Aug. Sept. Oct. Nov. Dec.

male

Dorsal (above)
orange dash
separated black stigma

Ventral (below)
contrasting gray fringe
pale spot band

Comments: The Little Glassywing is named for the translucent spots on the forewing. It regularly explores areas adjacent to its habitat. Adults have a low, quick flight and readily visit available flowers. It is not commonly encountered in home gardens. Males perch on low growing vegetation in sunny areas for females.

Little Glasswing
Pompeius verna

Family/Subfamily: Skippers (Hesperiidae)/ Banded Skippers (Hesperiinae)

Wingspan: 1.0–1.5" (2.5–3.8 cm)

Above: male is dark brown with black stigma and several semitransparent spots across forewing; female is dark brown with several semitransparent spots across forewing

Below: dark brown; hindwing purplish brown with band of faint, light spots

Sexes: similar; female darker with more rounded wings and larger forewing spots

Egg: white, laid singly on host leaves

Larva: green to greenish brown with dark mottling and stripes; head is reddish brown

Larval Host Plants: grasses including Purpletop Grass

Habitat: moist, open woodlands, forest edges, wetlands, roadsides, pastures, old fields and gardens

Broods: multiple generations

Abundance: occasional

Compare: Dun Skipper (pg. 105) similar in general size and color but ventral hindwing is typically unmarked and males lack semitransparent dorsal forewing spots.

Resident

Jan. Feb. Mar. Apr. May June July Aug. Sept. Oct. Nov. Dec.

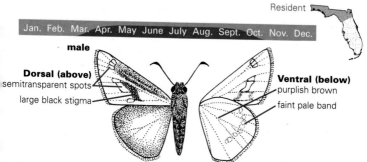

male

Dorsal (above)
semitransparent spots
large black stigma

Ventral (below)
purplish brown
faint pale band

Comments: Appearing more like a drab moth, the Carolina Satyr is a small brown butterfly with a low, weak flight. Common throughout the Southeast, the species shows up regularly in many residential yards. Between periodic bursts of activity, adults perch on grasses or leaf litter with their wings tightly closed. With care, they can be easily approached for observation. Males readily patrol for females.

Carolina Satyr
Hermeuptychia sosybius

Family/Subfamily: Brush-foots (Nymphalidae)/ Satyrs and Wood Nymphs (Satyrinae)

Wingspan: 1.0–1.5" (2.5–3.8 cm)

Above: dark brown with no distinct markings

Below: brown with narrow, dark brown submedian and postmedian lines; hindwing has row of yellow-rimmed dark eyespots

Sexes: similar

Egg: green, laid singly on host leaves

Larva: pale green with darker green longitudinal stripes and short yellow hairs

Larval Host Plants: various grasses including St. Augustine Grass

Habitat: woodlands and adjacent disturbed, grassy areas

Broods: multiple generations

Abundance: occasional to common

Compare: Viola's Wood Satyr (pg. 123) is larger and has large, yellow-rimmed dorsal and ventral eyespots.

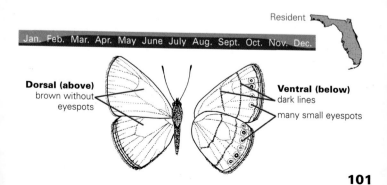

Resident

| Jan. | Feb. | Mar. | Apr. | May | June | July | Aug. | Sept. | Oct. | Nov. | Dec. |

Dorsal (above)
brown without eyespots

Ventral (below)
dark lines
many small eyespots

101

Larva

Comments: The Clouded Skipper is Florida's only member of this primarily tropical genus. Although superficially appearing drab, closer inspection is needed to appreciate the delicate lavender scaling on the hindwings below. It regularly explores the surrounding landscape and may show up occasionally in suburban yards or gardens. Adults have a quick, nervous flight but readily alight on low vegetation or leaf litter. It is an easy butterfly to approach.

Clouded Skipper
Lerema accius

Family/Subfamily: Skippers (Hesperiidae)/
Banded Skippers (Hesperiinae)

Wingspan: 1.0–1.5" (2.5–3.8 cm)

Above: dark chocolate brown; forewing has several
small semitransparent spots

Below: dark brown; forewing has row of small semitransparent spots near apex; both wings have lavender
scaling toward margin

Sexes: similar, female has larger forewing spots

Egg: laid singly on host leaves

Larva: green with a dark dorsal stripe and white lateral
stripes; head is white with a black margin and three
black stripes; body is covered with fine white spots

Larval Host Plants: various grasses including St.
Augustine Grass and Rustyseed Paspalum

Habitat: open woodlands, forest edges, roadsides, wetland edges, swamps, stream corridors and old fields

Broods: multiple generations

Abundance: occasional

Compare: Zabulon Skipper (pg. 141) female is similar in
coloration but has larger forewing spots and a white
bar along the top edge of the ventral hindwing.

Resident

Jan. Feb. Mar. Apr. May June July Aug. Sept. Oct. Nov. Dec.

male

Dorsal (above)
small semitransparent
spots

Ventral (below)
lavender sheen
dark central band

103

Male

Male Larva

Comments: The Dun Skipper is a small chocolate brown
butterfly with few markings. Although it prefers moist,
grassy or sedge-dominated areas associated with
deciduous woods, it frequently ventures into surrounding areas, and is periodically encountered in home
gardens. Adults have a quick, low flight and dart
around erratically over the vegetation. Males occasionally visit damp ground.

Dun Skipper
Euphyes vestris

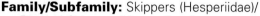

Family/Subfamily: Skippers (Hesperiidae)/
Banded Skippers (Hesperiinae)

Wingspan: 1.0–1.5" (2.5–3.8 cm)

Above: male is dark chocolate brown with black stigma;
female is dark brown with several whitish spots on
forewing

Below: brown; typically unmarked hindwing, but occasionally has faint spot band

Sexes: similar; female has small, white forewing spots

Egg: green, laid singly on host leaves

Larva: green with thin white lines; head is brown with
light outer stripes and dark center

Larval Host Plants: various sedges

Habitat: open woodlands, forest edges, roadsides, pastures, utility easements and old fields

Broods: two generations

Abundance: occasional

Compare: Little Glassywing (pg. 99) has distinct glassy
white spots on forewing and defined ventral hindwing
band.

Resident

Jan. Feb. Mar. Apr. May June July Aug. Sept. Oct. Nov. Dec.

male

Dorsal (above)
brown black wings
dark black stigma

Ventral (below)
unmarked or with faint
spot band

Comments: The Twin-Spot Skipper's unique pattern quickly distinguishes it from all other skippers in the state. It occasionally shows up in home gardens. Adults have a quick, darting flight but regularly alight on low vegetation. Little detailed information is known about the biology and behavior of this locally common butterfly.

Twin-Spot Skipper
Oligoria maculata

Family/Subfamily: Skippers (Hesperiidae)/
Banded Skippers (Hesperiinae)

Wingspan: 1.25–1.40" (3.2–3.6 cm)

Above: dark chocolate brown with small white spots
across forewing

Below: brown with three distinct white hindwing spots;
two close together and one isolated

Sexes: similar

Egg: brownish, laid singly on host leaves

Larva: pinkish green with brown head

Larval Host Plants: various grasses

Habitat: marshes, forest edges and pinelands

Broods: multiple generations

Abundance: occasional

Compare: Clouded Skipper (pg. 103) and Little
Glassywing (pg. 99) are similar in color but lack the distinct ventral hindwing white spots.

Resident

Jan. Feb. Mar. Apr. May June July Aug. Sept. Oct. Nov. Dec.

Dorsal (above)
white spots

Ventral (below)
brown with three
distinct white
spots: two next
to each other and
one separate

Ventral

Comments: The Southern Cloudywing frequents forest edges and open disturbed sites but is also a frequent garden visitor. Adults have a strong, erratic flight but frequently stop to nectar. Males perch on low vegetation and aggressively dart out to investigate intruders before returning to the same general location moments later. Adults rest with their wings partially open but are often rather nervous and difficult to closely approach.

Southern Cloudywing
Thorybes bathyllus

Family/Subfamily: Skippers (Hesperiidae)/ Spread-wing Skippers (Pyrginae)

Wingspan: 1.2–1.6" (3.0–4.1 cm)

Above: brown with straight, glassy white spots across forewing and light, checkered wing fringe; hindwing tapered slightly toward bottom

Below: brown; hindwing darker at base with two dark brown bands

Sexes: similar

Egg: green, laid singly on the leaves of host

Larva: greenish brown with black head, thin, dark dorsal stripe and narrow light lateral stripe; body covered with numerous short, light-colored hairs

Larval Host Plants: various legumes (Fabaceae) including beggarweeds, bush clovers, Butterfly Pea and Hog Peanut

Habitat: open, disturbed sites including roadsides, old fields, utility easements and forest edges

Broods: multiple generations

Abundance: occasional to common

Compare: Northern Cloudywing (pg. 111) and Confused Cloudywing (*Thorybes confusis*) are similar in size and appearance, but their smaller white dorsal forewing spots do not form a distinct band.

Resident

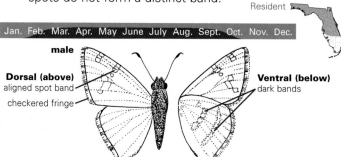

Jan. Feb. Mar. Apr. May June July Aug. Sept. Oct. Nov. Dec.

male

Dorsal (above)
aligned spot band
checkered fringe

Ventral (below)
dark bands

Comments: The Northern Cloudywing is one of several similar-looking and closely related dark brown skippers found in Florida. The butterfly has a low, skipping flight and quickly darts along trails or clearings occasionally stopping to nectar. It readily visits nearby gardens. Males perch on the ground or low on vegetation and quickly speed out to engage rival males or passing females. At rest, they hold their wings in a relaxed, partially open position.

Northern Cloudywing
Thorybes pylades

Family/Subfamily: Skippers (Hesperiidae)/
Spread-wing Skippers (Pyrginae)

Wingspan: 1.2–1.7" (3.0–4.3 cm)

Above: brown with several small, elongated, misaligned
glassy white spots on forewing and light, checkered
wing fringe

Below: brown; hindwing darker at base with two dark
brown bands; forewing has lavender scaling toward
apex

Sexes: similar

Egg: pale greenish white, laid singly on the leaves of
host

Larva: greenish brown with black head, thin, dark dorsal
stripe and narrow pinkish brown lateral stripe; body
covered with numerous short, light-colored hairs

Larval Host Plants: various legumes including beggarweeds, bush clovers, Butterfly Pea and milk vetch

Habitat: open woodlands, forest clearings, forest edges,
roadsides, utility easements and old fields

Broods: multiple generations

Abundance: occasional to common

Compare: Southern Cloudywing (pg. 109) has larger
white dorsal forewing spots that form distinct band.

Resident

Jan. Feb. Mar. Apr. May June July Aug. Sept. Oct. Nov. Dec.

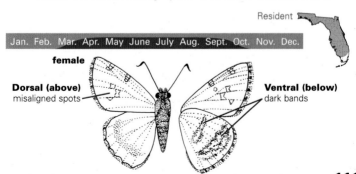

female

Dorsal (above)
misaligned spots

Ventral (below)
dark bands

111

Male

Female Larva

Comments: A common spring species, Juvenal's Duskywing darts up and down sunlit trails and explores adjacent open sites with a quick, low flight. It frequently visits flowers or basks on bare ground with wings spread. Males perch on low vegetation and actively pursue passing objects. They occasionally puddle at damp sand or gravel. The larvae construct individual shelters on the host by folding over leaves with silk.

Juvenal's Duskywing
Erynnis juvenalis

Family/Subfamily: Skippers (Hesperiidae)/
Spread-wing Skippers (Pyrginae)

Wingspan: 1.20–1.75" (3.0–4.4 cm)

Above: dark brown; forewing has small cluster of tiny
clear spots near wingtip and one at end of cell, and is
heavily patterned with brown, gray, black and tan;
female has increased gray scaling and heavier pattern

Below: brown, lightening toward wing margin; hindwing
has two small, light spots along leading margin

Sexes: similar, although female is lighter and more heavily patterned with larger forewing spots

Egg: pale green, laid singly on host leaves

Larva: pale green with thin, light lateral stripe and reddish brown head; head capsule has outer row of light
orange spots

Larval Host Plants: various oaks including White Oak,
Post Oak and Black Oak

Habitat: oak woodlands, forest edges, woodland clearings, roadsides and utility easements

Broods: single generation

Abundance: occasional to common

Compare: Horace's Duskywing (pg. 117) lacks two light
spots on hindwing beneath.

Resident

Jan. Feb. Mar. Apr. May June July Aug. Sept. Oct. Nov. Dec.

male

Dorsal (above)
glassy spot at end
of cell

small glassy spots

gray scaling

Ventral (below)
two round light spots
along margin

113

Larva

Comments: Often overlooked, the Gemmed Satyr is
one of the most attractive members of the subfamily
Satyrinae (satyrs and wood nymphs) in Florida with its
beautifully marked hindwings. It is the only Florida
satyr without eyespots. It dances along the forest floor
with a weak, low flight. Although difficult to follow
through the understory vegetation, adults regularly
alight on grass blades or leaf litter. The slender larvae
have both a green and brown form.

Gemmed Satyr
Cyllopsis gemma

Family/Subfamily: Brush-foots (Nymphalidae)/ Satyrs and Wood Nymphs (Satyrinae)

Wingspan: 1.25–1.70" (3.2–4.3 cm)

Above: light brown with very small dark spots along hindwing margin

Below: light speckled brown with large purplish hindwing patch containing black spots with silver highlights

Sexes: similar

Egg: green, laid singly on host leaves

Larva: green or brown with thin pale stripes, two small tails and two brownish pink horns on the head

Larval Host Plants: Bermuda Grass and other grasses

Habitat: moist woodlands and associated shady grassy areas

Broods: two or more generations

Abundance: occasional; locally common

Compare: Similar in color and relative size to the Carolina Satyr (pg. 101) and Viola's Wood Satyr (pg. 123) but lacks yellow-rimmed ventral hindwing eye-spots.

Resident

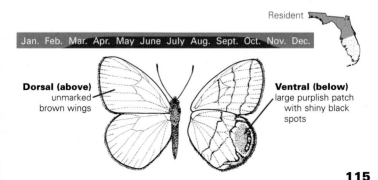

Jan. Feb. Mar. Apr. May June July Aug. Sept. Oct. Nov. Dec.

Dorsal (above)
unmarked
brown wings

Ventral (below)
large purplish patch
with shiny black
spots

115

Male

Female Larva

Comments: This abundant skipper commonly wanders into disturbed sites near its habitat in search of nectar. It is often a common garden visitor. It holds its wings outstretched when feeding or at rest. Adults flutter about with quick, somewhat erratic flight usually low to the ground. Males perch on low vegetation and occasionally puddle at damp sand or gravel. The larvae construct individual shelters on the host by folding over leaves with silk. Once fully mature, the larvae from the late season generation overwinter among the leaf litter until the following spring.

Horace's Duskywing
Erynnis horatius

Family/Subfamily: Skippers (Hesperiidae)/
Spread-wing Skippers (Pyrginae)

Wingspan: 1.25–1.75" (3.2–4.4 cm)

Above: dark brown overall with gray scaling usually lacking; forewing has cluster of small clear spots near wingtip and distinctive clear spot at end of forewing cell; female is lighter with more contrasting pattern; clear spots typically larger than in most other duskywings

Below: brown with faint rows of light spots along outer edge of hindwing

Sexes: similar, although female is lighter with more heavily patterned forewings and larger forewing spots

Egg: pale yellow green, laid singly on new growth of host

Larva: pale green with tiny white spots and a reddish orange head

Larval Host Plants: various oaks including Live Oak, Turkey Oak, Water Oak and Myrtle Oak

Habitat: oak woodlands, oak scrub, forest edges, woodland clearings, roadsides and utility easements

Broods: multiple generations

Abundance: occasional to common

Compare: Juvenal's Duskywing (pg. 113) has two light spots along upper margin of ventral hindwing and gray scaling on dorsal forewing.

Resident

Jan. Feb. Mar. Apr. May June July Aug. Sept. Oct. Nov. Dec.

male

Dorsal (above)
glassy spots
glassy spot at end
of cell

Ventral (below)
lacks spots along
leading margin

Dorsal

Comments: The Hoary Edge readily ventures into disturbed sites near its habitat and shows up occasionally in home gardens. Limited to northern portions of the state, it is frequently sighted but rarely found in any large numbers. Adults have a low, strong flight and can be a challenge to follow. Males perch on low, protruding vegetation and aggressively investigate and chase passing insects.

Hoary Edge
Achalarus lyciades

Family/Subfamily: Skippers (Hesperiidae)/ Spread-wing Skippers (Pyrginae)

Wingspan: 1.40–1.75" (3.6–4.4 cm)

Above: brown with broad band of gold spots across forewing and checkered fringe

Below: brown; forewing as above but muted; hindwing mottled dark brown at base with distinct broad white marginal patch

Sexes: similar

Egg: cream, laid singly on host leaves

Larva: dark green; covered with numerous tiny pale yellow dots; has a thin, brownish orange lateral stripe and black head

Larval Host Plants: beggarweeds

Habitat: open, sandy woodlands, forest edges and adjacent disturbed, brushy areas

Broods: two generations

Abundance: occasional

Compare: Silver-Spotted Skipper (pg. 137) is larger, has white median ventral hindwing patch and round, stubby tail.

Resident

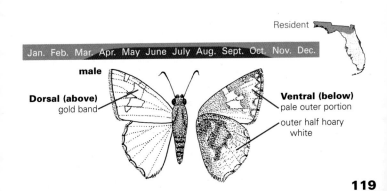

Jan. Feb. Mar. Apr. May June July Aug. Sept. Oct. Nov. Dec.

male

Dorsal (above)
gold band

Ventral (below)
pale outer portion

outer half hoary white

Larva

Comments: Unusually colorful, the Georgia Satyr tends to be less frequently encountered than most of its common cousins. Adults have a low, weak flight and bob slowly among the tall grasses and surrounding vegetation. Although often localized and spotty in distribution, the butterfly cannot be confused with any other satyr or wood nymph in the state. Little detailed information is available about the biology and behavior of the species including the exact larval hosts utilized in the wild.

Georgia Satyr
Neonympha areolata

Family/Subfamily: Brush-foots (Nymphalidae)/
Satyrs and Wood Nymphs (Satyrinae)

Wingspan: 1.40–1.75" (3.6–4.4 cm)

Above: brown with no pattern elements

Below: light brown with distinct reddish orange lines;
hindwing has a row of elongated yellow-rimmed eyespots encircled in a thin reddish orange oval

Sexes: similar

Egg: pale green to yellow, laid singly on host leaves

Larva: green with narrow light stripes, two short tails
and two reddish horns on the head.

Larval Host Plants: unknown; various sedges likely,
will accept grasses in captivity

Habitat: open, moist, grassy areas, wet meadows, pine
savannahs, roadsides

Broods: one or more generations

Abundance: occasional

Compare: Carolina Satyr (pg. 101), Viola's Wood Satyr
(pg. 123) and Gemmed Satyr (pg. 115) are similar in
size and ground coloration but lack distinct red orange
ventral markings and oval hindwing eyespot.

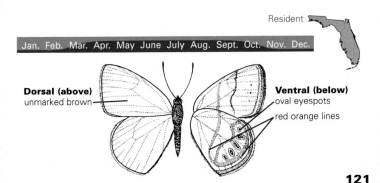

Resident

Jan. Feb. Mar. Apr. May June July Aug. Sept. Oct. Nov. Dec.

Dorsal (above)
unmarked brown

Ventral (below)
oval eyespots
red orange lines

Comments: Viola's Wood Satyr scurries along the forest floor with a quick, bobbing flight and periodically lands on leaf litter or low vegetation with wings tightly closed. Like most satyrs, it does not visit flowers but instead is drawn to sap flows and rotting fruit. The large yellow-rimmed eyespots presumably help deflect attack away from the insect's vulnerable body. With even a good portion of its wing missing, the butterfly can still fly and will live to see another day.

Viola's Wood Satyr
Megisto viola

Family/Subfamily: Brush-foots (Nymphalidae)/ Satyrs and Wood Nymphs (Satyrinae)

Wingspan: 1.3–1.9" (3.3–4.8 cm)

Above: brown with large yellow-rimmed eyespots on both wings; male has two conspicuous eyespots on the forewing and one to two on the hindwing; female has two or three on the hindwing

Below: light brown with a dark brown submedian and postmedian lines and large, yellow-rimmed eyespots; silver markings between eyespots

Sexes: similar, although female has larger eyespots

Egg: green, laid singly on host leaves

Larva: brown with dark dorsal stripe and two stubby tails

Larval Host Plants: various grasses including St. Augustine Grass

Habitat: shady woodlands, forest edges and adjacent open areas

Broods: single spring generation

Abundance: occasional to common

Compare: Carolina Satyr (pg. 101) is smaller and lacks large, yellow-rimmed dorsal eyespots.

Resident

Jan. Feb. Mar. Apr. May June July Aug. Sept. Oct. Nov. Dec.

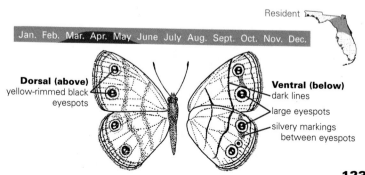

Dorsal (above)
yellow-rimmed black eyespots

Ventral (below)
dark lines
large eyespots
silvery markings between eyespots

123

Ventral

Larva

Comments: Although only recently established in Florida, the Dorantes Skipper is now a common butterfly of forest edges and adjacent open, disturbed sites. Adults have a quick, darting flight and are frequently drawn to available flowers. It is often abundant in home gardens. Like several other members of the family, the larvae construct individual shelters on the host by weaving together one or more leaves with silk. Adults are found throughout the year and survive the winter in reproductive diapause.

Dorantes Skipper
Urbanus dorantes

Family/Subfamily: Skippers (Hesperiidae)/
Spread-wing Skippers (Pyrginae)

Wingspan: 1.4–1.8" (3.6–4.6 cm)

Above: brown with several semitransparent spots on
forewing and long hindwing tail

Below: brown; hindwing has two more diffuse dark
brown bands

Sexes: similar

Egg: green, laid singly on the leaves of host

Larva: yellow-green with pinkish hue and a black head;
body has a thin dark dorsal stripe and lateral band of
dark-rimmed pale yellow spots

Larval Host Plants: various legumes including beggarweeds

Habitat: open woodlands, roadsides, old fields, fallow
agricultural land, utility easements, forest edges and
gardens

Broods: multiple generations

Abundance: occasional to common

Compare: Long-Tailed Skipper (pg. 129) has dorsal
greenish blue sheen.

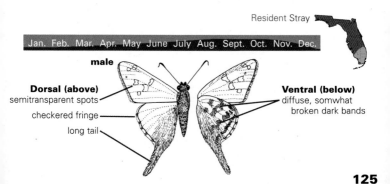

Resident Stray

Jan. Feb. Mar. Apr. May June July Aug. Sept. Oct. Nov. Dec.

male

Dorsal (above)
semitransparent spots

checkered fringe

long tail

Ventral (below)
diffuse, somwhat
broken dark bands

125

Comments: Freshly emerged Ocola Skippers often have a noticeable purplish sheen to the hindwings below. The butterfly can be encountered in a wide range of habitats including suburban gardens. Adults have a fast, darting flight typically within a few feet of the ground. It is a year-round resident of the state and is particularly abundant toward the end of summer.

Ocola Skipper
Panoquina ocola

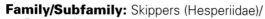

Family/Subfamily: Skippers (Hesperiidae)/
Banded Skippers (Hesperiinae)

Wingspan: 1.50–1.75" (3.8–4.4 cm)

Above: elongated and slender wings; brown with pale
median forewing spots

Below: brown with light veins and a subtle purple sheen;
typically darker toward margin; often has faint postmedian spot band

Sexes: similar

Egg: green, laid singly on host leaves

Larva: light green with yellow stripes and green head

Larval Host Plants: various grasses including Southern
Cutgrass

Habitat: marshes, pond margins, forest edges, roadsides, old fields, utility easements and gardens

Broods: multiple generations

Abundance: occasional to common

Compare: Salt Marsh Skipper (pg. 93) is lighter brown
beneath with distinct light, wide veins. Brazilian
Skipper (pg. 133) is similar in color and appearance but
has row of semitransparent spots on ventral hindwing.

Resident

Jan. Feb. Mar. Apr. May June July Aug. Sept. Oct. Nov. Dec.

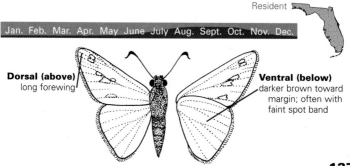

Dorsal (above)
long forewing

Ventral (below)
darker brown toward
margin; often with
faint spot band

Ventral

Larva

Comments: The Long-tailed Skipper is one of the most common and distinctive skippers in Florida and resembles a small swallowtail. Adults have a quick, low flight. They are fond of flowers and often abundant in home gardens. The larvae construct individual shelters on the host by folding over small sections of a leaf with silk. Older larvae may use the entire leaf or connect several leaves together. The butterfly is migratory, and moves southward each fall to overwinter in warmer portions of the state.

Long-Tailed Skipper
Urbanus proteus

Family/Subfamily: Skippers (Hesperiidae)/
Spread-wing Skippers (Pyrginae)

Wingspan: 1.5–2.0" (3.8–5.1 cm)

Above: brown with iridescent blue-green scaling on wing
bases and body; long hindwing tail; forewing has several semitransparent spots

Below: brown; hindwing has two crisp dark brown bands

Sexes: similar

Egg: pale yellow, laid singly on the underside of host
leaves

Larva: yellow-green with a dark dorsal stripe, yellow lateral stripe and crimson head; body is covered with tiny
black spots

Larval Host Plants: a wide variety of legumes including beggarweeds, wisteria and Kudzu

Habitat: open, disturbed sites including roadsides, old
fields, fallow agricultural land, utility easements, forest
edges and gardens

Broods: multiple generations

Abundance: common to abundant

Compare: Dorantes Skipper (pg. 125) is very similar in
size and appearance but lacks iridescent blue-green
dorsal coloration.

Resident

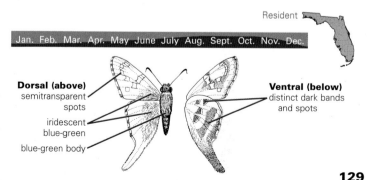

Jan. Feb. Mar. Apr. May June July Aug. Sept. Oct. Nov. Dec.

Dorsal (above)
semitransparent
spots

iridescent
blue-green

blue-green body

Ventral (below)
distinct dark bands
and spots

129

Larva

Comments: The American Snout gets its name from the
unusually long labial palpi that resemble an elongated
nose. This unique feature, combined with the cryptic
coloration of the wings beneath enhances the butterfly's overall "dead leaf" appearance when at rest.
Adults have a rapid, somewhat erratic flight and are
commonly drawn to flowers. Males readily puddle at
damp ground. Although often common, it is seldom
encountered in large numbers.

American Snout
Libytheana carinenta

Family/Subfamily: Brush-foots (Nymphalidae)/ Snouts (Libytheinae)

Wingspan: 1.6–1.9" (4.1–4.8 cm)

Above: brown with orange patches and white forewing spots

Below: brown with orange basal forewing scaling and white spots; hindwing variable; plain brown or pinkish brown with heavy mottling

Sexes: similar

Egg: tiny white eggs laid in axils of host leaves

Larva: light green with numerous small yellow dots and yellow lateral stripe; thorax has two small black eye-spots

Larval Host Plants: Common Hackberry and Sugarberry

Habitat: rich, deciduous woodlands, stream corridors, forest edges and adjacent open areas

Broods: multiple generations

Abundance: occasional to common

Compare: unique

Resident

Jan. Feb. Mar. Apr. May June July Aug. Sept. Oct. Nov. Dec.

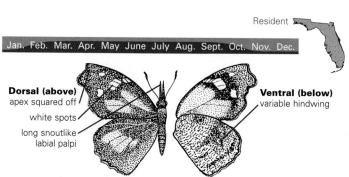

Dorsal (above)
apex squared off
white spots
long snoutlike labial palpi

Ventral (below)
variable hindwing

131

Dorsal

Larva

Comments: The Brazilian Skipper is also referred to as the Canna Skipper and can be a common nuisance or aesthetic pest on ornamental cannas in home and commercial landscapes. The alien-looking, transparent larvae construct individual shelters by rolling over sections of the host leaf with silk. Inside they hide safely out of the sight of would-be predators and come out to feed mainly at night. The adults have a strong, rapid flight, usually low to the ground, and visit a wide range of flowers. Primarily a tropical butterfly, it is unable to survive freezing temperatures in any life stage.

Brazilian Skipper
Calpodes ethlius

Family/Subfamily: Skippers (Hesperiidae)/
Banded Skippers (Hesperiinae)

Wingspan: 1.75–2.25" (4.4–5.7 cm)

Above: brown elongated wings with several semitransparent spots across forewing; hindwing has central
band of three small semitransparent spots; hindwing
tapers toward bottom

Below: as above but lighter brown

Sexes: similar

Egg: gray-green, laid singly on host leaves

Larva: green, semitransparent with orange-brown head;
head has a central black dot

Larval Host Plants: cannas

Habitat: marshes, pond edges, parks, gardens and various urban areas

Broods: multiple generations

Abundance: occasional to common

Compare: Ocola Skipper (pg. 127) is similar in appearance but smaller and lacks ventral hindwing band of
semitransparent spots.

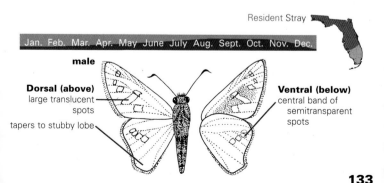

Resident Stray

Jan. Feb. Mar. Apr. May June July Aug. Sept. Oct. Nov. Dec.

male

Dorsal (above)
large translucent
spots

tapers to stubby lobe

Ventral (below)
central band of
semitransparent
spots

Ventral

Larva

Comments: The Southern Pearly Eye is Florida's largest satyr. Adults have a quick, bobbing flight and frequently alight on low vegetation or leaf litter. The butterfly has a spotty distribution but may be locally abundant when found. Like most satyrs, adults do not visit flowers. They instead prefer to feed at sap flows, rotting fruit, decaying vegetation and dung.

Southern Pearly Eye
Enodia portlandia

Family/Subfamily: Brush-foots (Nymphalidae)/
Satyrs and Wood Nymphs (Satyrinae)

Wingspan: 1.75–2.25" (4.4–5.7 cm)

Above: light brown; wings have eyespots on light postmedian patch

Below: purplish brown; hindwing has submarginal cream
band and row of yellow-rimmed dark eyespots

Sexes: similar, although females generally somewhat
lighter in color

Egg: pale green, laid singly on host leaves

Larva: green with narrow light stripes, two short tails
and two reddish horns on the head

Larval Host Plants: Giant Cane

Habitat: moist woodland and stream corridors

Broods: multiple generations

Abundance: occasional; localized

Compare: Much larger than Viola's Wood Satyr (pg. 123)
with numerous dark eyespots on ventral hindwing.

Resident

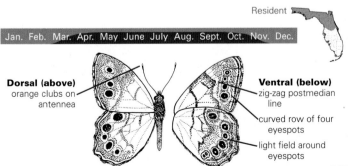

Jan. Feb. Mar. Apr. May June July Aug. Sept. Oct. Nov. Dec.

Dorsal (above)
orange clubs on
antennea

Ventral (below)
zig-zag postmedian
line

curved row of four
eyespots

light field around
eyespots

135

Larva

Comments: The Silver-spotted Skipper is a large, robust butterfly with a rapid, darting flight. It is a common garden visitor. They have a long proboscis and can easily gain access to nectar from a variety of flowers. Males perch on shrubs or overhanging branches and aggressively investigate passersby. The colorful larvae construct individual shelters on the host by tying one or more leaves together with silk.

Silver-spotted Skipper
Epargyreus clarus

Family/Subfamily: Skippers (Hesperiidae)/
Spread-wing Skippers (Pyrginae)

Wingspan: 1.75–2.40" (4.4–6.1 cm)

Above: brown with median row of gold spots on
forewing and checkered wing fringe; hindwing is
tapered into small, rounded tail

Below: brown; forewing as above; hindwing has distinct,
elongated silver-white patch in center

Sexes: similar

Egg: green, laid singly on host leaves

Larva: yellow-green with dark bands and reddish brown
head

Larval Host Plants: wide variety of Fabaceous plants
including wisteria, False Indigo, Kudzu, Butterfly Pea
and beggarweeds

Habitat: forest edges, open woodlands, roadsides, utility
easements, old fields and gardens

Broods: multiple generations

Abundance: occasional to common

Compare: Hoary Edge (pg. 119) is smaller and has marginal white ventral hindwing patch.

Resident

Jan. Feb. Mar. Apr. May June July Aug. Sept. Oct. Nov. Dec.

male

Dorsal (above)
pointed forewing
gold spots
lobe

Ventral (below)
wide silver-white
patch

Female

Ventral

Larva

Comments: The Common Buckeye is one of the most easily identified butterflies. Its large, target-shaped eyespots help deflect predation away from the insects' vulnerable body. It is fond of open, sunny locations with low-growing vegetation. Adults frequently alight on bare soil or gravel but are extremely wary and difficult to approach. Males readily establish territories and actively investigate passing objects. Flight is rapid and low to the ground. Unable to withstand freezing temperatures in any life stage, the Buckeye annually undertakes a southward fall migration and overwinters in warmer Gulf Coast locations including Florida.

Common Buckeye
Junonia coenia

Family/Subfamily: Brushfoots (Nymphalidae)/
True Brush-foots (Nymphalinae)

Wingspan: 1.5–2.7" (3.8–6.9 cm)

Above: brown with prominent eyespots; forewing bears
a distinct white patch and two small orange bars

Below: forewing has prominent white band; hindwings
seasonally variable in color; summer forms are light
brown with numerous pattern elements; cool-season
forms are reddish brown with reduced markings

Sexes: similar, although female has broader wings and
larger hindwing eyespots

Egg: dark green, laid singly on host leaves

Larva: black with lateral white stripes, orange patches
and branched spines

Larval Host Plants: plants in many families including
toadflax, False Foxglove, plantain and twinflower

Habitat: fields, pastures, roadsides, pineland, disturbed
sites

Broods: multiple generations, overwinters as adult

Abundance: occasional to locally common, abundant in
fall

Compare: Mangrove Buckeye (pg. 149) is often larger
and has pale orange dorsal forewing bands.

Resident

Jan. Feb. Mar. Apr. May June July Aug. Sept. Oct. Nov. Dec.

Dorsal (above)
white band that
wraps eyespot

orange bars

eyespots

orange band

Ventral (below)
seasonally variable

Female

Male pg. 199   Female   Male

Comments: Sexually dimorphic, the Zabulon Skipper is a
   small butterfly with a bright orange male and a drab
   brown female. It occasionally wanders into suburban
   gardens. Adults have a rapid flight and are strongly
   attracted to flowers. Males perch on sunlit branches
   along trails or clearings and engage passing objects or
   rival males. Females generally prefer to remain within
   the confines of nearby shady sites.

Zabulon Skipper
Poanes zabulon

Family/Subfamily: Skippers (Hesperiidae)/
Banded Skippers (Hesperiinae)

Wingspan: 1.0–1.4" (2.5–3.6 cm)

Above: male is golden orange with dark brown borders
and small brown spot near forewing apex; female is
dark brown with band of cream spots across forewing

Below: male hindwing yellow with brown base and margin enclosing a yellow spot; female is dark brown with
small band of light spots near forewing apex, lavender
scaling on wing margins, and white band along apex

Sexes: dissimilar, female brown with little orange color

Egg: pale green, laid singly on host leaves

Larva: tan with dark dorsal stripe, white lateral stripe and
reddish brown head; body is covered with short, light-
colored hairs

Larval Host Plants: various grasses including
Purpletop Grass and lovegrass

Habitat: open woodlands, forest edges, roadsides, pastures, wetland edges, stream corridors and old fields

Broods: two generations

Abundance: occasional

Compare: Clouded Skipper (pg. 103) lacks large dorsal
forewing spots and white band along the top margin
of the ventral hindwing.

Resident

Jan. Feb. Mar. Apr. May June July Aug. Sept. Oct. Nov. Dec.

male

Dorsal (above)
dark spot
golden orange

Ventral (below)
dark base encloses
yellow spot
yellow with spots

141

Male

Ventral

Larva

Comments: The Hackberry Butterfly has a strong, rapid
flight and rarely ventures out into open areas. Males
readily establish territories. They perch on sunlit
leaves, overhanging branches or tree trunks along forest trails and woodland edges, and dart out to engage
passing objects or make exploratory flights. Adults are
drawn to sap flows or rotting fruit. Although often
spotty in distribution, the species can be relatively
abundant when encountered.

Hackberry Butterfly
Asterocampa celtis

Family/Subfamily: Brush-foots (Nymphalidae)/
Emperors (Apaturinae)

Wingspan: 2.0–2.6" (5.1–6.6 cm)

Above: amber-brown with dark markings and borders;
forewing bears several small white spots near the
apex and a single submarginal black eyespot; hindwing
has a postmedian row of dark spots

Below: as above with muted coloration; hindwing has
postmedian row of yellow-rimmed black spots with
blue green centers

Sexes: similar, although female has broader wings

Egg: cream-white, laid singly or in small clusters on host
leaves

Larva: light green with two narrow dorsal yellow stripes
and mottled with small yellow spots; head is dark and
bears two stubby, branched horns; rear end has a pair
of short tails

Larval Host Plants: Sugarberry

Habitat: rich, shady woodlands and forest margins

Broods: multiple generations

Abundance: occasional

Compare: Tawny Emperor (pg. 147) is more orange-
brown above and lacks white forewing spots and
single forewing eyespot.

Resident

Jan. Feb. Mar. Apr. May June July Aug. Sept. Oct. Nov. Dec.

Dorsal (above)
white spots
single eyespot
one bar
two spots
row of dark spots

Ventral (below)
eyespots with blue
green centers

143

Comments: The Common Wood Nymph is a medium-sized butterfly primarily encountered in open, grassy meadows and fields, though it may also be found in forest clearings and margins. Within the state, it is infrequent and often highly localized. Adults have a low, relaxed flight and bob erratically through the vegetation. Well camouflaged when resting, it can be a challenge to locate or follow. Unlike most satyrs, it is an opportunistic feeder and frequently visits flowers along with sap flows and fermenting fruit.

Common Wood Nymph
Cercyonis pegala

Family/Subfamily: Brush-foots (Nymphalidae)/
Satyrs and Wood Nymphs (Satyrinae)

Wingspan: 1.8–2.8" (4.6–7.1 cm)

Above: brown; forewing has large postmedian yellow
patch containing two dark eyespots

Below: brown with dark striations; forewing has large
postmedian yellow patch containing two dark eyespots; hindwing has postmedian row of small,
yellow-rimmed dark eyespots

Sexes: similar, although female is paler and has larger
eyespots

Egg: cream, laid singly on host leaves

Larva: green with dark green dorsal stripe and light side
stripes

Larval Host Plants: various grasses

Habitat: open woodlands, forest edges, marshes, grassy
fields and roadsides

Broods: single generation

Abundance: occasional

Compare: Viola's Wood Satyr (pg. 123) is smaller and
lacks large yellow forewing patch.

Resident

Jan. Feb. Mar. Apr. May June July Aug. Sept. Oct. Nov. Dec.

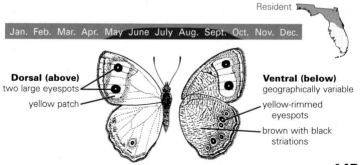

Dorsal (above)
two large eyespots
yellow patch

Ventral (below)
geographically variable
yellow-rimmed
eyespots
brown with black
striations

Male | Female | Larva

Comments: The Tawny Emperor is superficially similar to the Hackberry Butterfly with which it flies. Adults are rapid, strong fliers and often difficult to approach. Males perch on sunlit leaves or on the sides of large trees and dart out quickly to investigate passing objects. The developing larvae remain together and feed communally through the first three instars before becoming more solitary.

Tawny Emperor
Asterocampa clyton

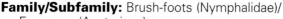

Family/Subfamily: Brush-foots (Nymphalidae)/ Emperors (Apaturinae)

Wingspan: 2.00–2.75" (5.1–7.0 cm)

Above: orange-brown with dark markings and borders; hindwing has a postmedian row of dark spots

Below: as above with muted gray-brown cast and dark-rimmed hindwing eyespots

Sexes: similar, although female much larger with broader, rounder wings; male has narrowed, triangular wings

Egg: cream-white, laid in large pyramidal clusters on the underside of host leaves

Larva: light green with broad dorsal yellow stripes, narrow yellow lateral stripes and mottled with small yellow spots; head is green and bears two stubby, branched horns; rear end has a pair of short tails

Larval Host Plants: Sugarberry

Habitat: rich woodlands, forest edges and adjacent areas

Broods: multiple generations

Abundance: occasional; locally abundant

Compare: Hackberry Butterfly (pg. 143) is lighter brown with single black dorsal forewing spot and white spots near forewing apex.

Resident

Jan. Feb. Mar. Apr. May June July Aug. Sept. Oct. Nov. Dec.

Dorsal (above)
no white spots
no black eyespot
two bars

Ventral (below)
muted pattern

147

Female

Female ventral

Comments: The Mangrove Buckeye is found throughout the Keys and coastal areas of the southern mainland, and is locally abundant. Adults have a low, rapid flight and often alight on bare soil or low vegetation. Males establish territories and actively investigate passing intruders. Adults can be found year-round.

Mangrove Buckeye
Junonia evarete

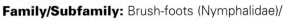

Family/Subfamily: Brush-foots (Nymphalidae)/
True Brush-foots (Nymphalinae)

Wingspan: 2.00–2.75" (5.1–7.0 cm)

Above: brown with light orange forewing band and sub-marginal hindwing band; forewing has a prominent dark eyespot and two orange bars in cell; hindwing bears two large eyespots

Below: forewing as above with muted markings; hindwing brown with faint pattern elements and small eyespots

Sexes: similar, although female has broader wings and larger hindwing eyespots

Egg: green, laid singly on host leaves

Larva: black with cream and blue markings and numerous branched spines

Larval Host Plants: Black Mangrove

Habitat: coastal mangroves, salt marshes and adjacent open areas

Broods: multiple generations

Abundance: occasional; locally abundant

Compare: Common Buckeye (pg. 139) is smaller and has white forewing band surrounding forewing eyespot.

Resident

Jan. Feb. Mar. Apr. May June July Aug. Sept. Oct. Nov. Dec.

male

Dorsal (above)

pale orange
forewing band

eyespot ringed
with orange

hindwing eyespots
similar in size

Ventral (below)

149

Ventral

Comments: The Yucca Giant-Skipper is a beautifully marked butterfly with elongated wings. Adults have a rapid, powerful flight that produces a noticeable buzz. Males perch on vegetation along trails or clearings and actively defend their territory. The butterfly is particularly active in late afternoon or early evening. The larvae feed on host leaves when young but soon burrow into stem and large taproot, forming a long tunnel.

Yucca Giant-Skipper
Megathymus yuccae

Family/Subfamily: Skippers (Hesperiidae)/ Giant-Skippers (Megathyminae)

Wingspan: 2.0–2.8" (5.1–7.1 cm)

Above: blackish brown with yellow hindwing border and band of yellow spots on forewing; small white patch near the forewing apex; female has small postmedian band of tiny orange spots on hindwing

Below: chocolate brown with marginal frosting and distinct white patch along upper margin of hindwing

Sexes: similar, although female is significantly larger with broader wings and an additional row of yellow spots on hindwing

Egg: pinkish brown, laid singly on host leaves

Larva: light tan with reddish brown head

Larval Host Plants: yuccas

Habitat: dry woodlands, pinelands and scrub

Broods: single generation

Abundance: occasional; local

Compare: Cofaqui Giant-Skipper (*Megathymus cofaqui*) is duller gray-brown below with less prominent scattered small white ventral hindwing spots.

Resident

Jan. Feb. Mar. Apr. May June July Aug. Sept. Oct. Nov. Dec.

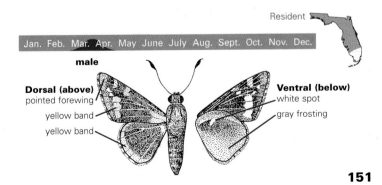

male

Dorsal (above)
pointed forewing
yellow band
yellow band

Ventral (below)
white spot
gray frosting

151

Male

Male ventral Larva

Comments: Originally described in 1911 by William Schaus, a physician visiting Miami to treat yellow fever victims, this swallowtail is one of the rarest butterflies in Florida. Once found throughout much of Keys and extreme southern portions of the mainland, its range and population numbers have been severely reduced over the past half-century due to habitat loss and mosquito control pesticide use. Today, the butterfly remains primarily restricted to the intact hardwood hammocks of northern Key Largo and the islands within Biscayne National Park. Schaus' Swallowtail is Florida's only federally endangered butterfly.

Schaus' Swallowtail
Papilio aristodemus ponceanus

Family/Subfamily: Swallowtails (Papilionidae)/ Swallowtails (Papilioninae)

Wingspan: 3.25–5.25" (8.3–13.3 cm)

Above: dark brown with a submarginal row of yellow spots and a broad yellow median band; hindwing tails outlined in yellow

Below: yellow with brown markings and wide reddish brown median hindwing band bordered by a row of blue spots

Sexes: similar, although male has yellow-tipped antennae

Egg: light or dark green, laid singly on host leaves; new growth is strongly preferred

Larva: brown with cream and yellow patches and several longitudinal rows of blue spots; young larvae resemble bird droppings

Larval Host Plants: Wild Lime and Torchwood

Habitat: tropical hardwood hammock

Broods: single generation

Abundance: rare; highly localized; state and federally endangered

Compare: Giant Swallowtail (pg. 155) is generally larger, has yellow-centered hindwing tails, and intersecting yellow forewing bands.

Resident

Jan. Feb. Mar. Apr. May June July Aug. Sept. Oct. Nov. Dec.

Dorsal (above)
broad diagonal yellow band

tails are black edged with yellow

Ventral (below)
reddish brown band edged in blue

Male

Ventral Larva

Comments: Living up to its name, the Giant Swallowtail is one of the largest butterflies in Florida. The impressive adults are strong fliers but readily stop at colorful flowering plants to feed and are regular garden visitors. When nectaring, adults continuously flutter their wings much like a hummingbird. This behavior coupled with a long proboscis enables them to visit a wide range of flowers, including many that otherwise might not easily support their weight. Giant Swallowtail larvae, often called "orange dogs" because of their fondness for citrus, occasionally become minor pests in commercial orange groves.

Giant Swallowtail
Papilio cresphontes

Family/Subfamily: Swallowtails (Papilionidae)/ Swallowtails (Papilioninae)

Wingspan: 4.5–5.5" (11.4–14.0 cm)

Above: chocolate brown with broad bands of yellow spots; characteristic diagonal band extends from tip of forewing to base of abdomen; hindwing tail has yellow center

Below: cream yellow with brown markings and blue median hindwing band

Sexes: similar, although females generally much larger

Egg: amber-brown, laid singly on upperside of host leaves

Larva: brown with yellow and cream patches; resembles bird dropping

Larval Host Plants: Hercules Club, Wild Lime, Wafer Ash and various cultivated citrus species

Habitat: woodlands, pastures, forest edges, orange groves, suburban gardens

Broods: multiple generations, late February to November northward and year-round in southern portions

Abundance: occasional

Compare: Schaus' Swallowtail (pg. 153) is smaller and lacks yellow spot in center of hindwing tail.

Resident

Jan. Feb. Mar. Apr. May June July Aug. Sept. Oct. Nov. Dec.

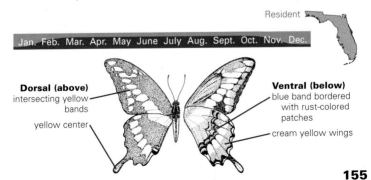

Dorsal (above)
intersecting yellow bands

yellow center

Ventral (below)
blue band bordered with rust-colored patches

cream yellow wings

155

Comments: The Red-banded Hairstreak has a rapid, erratic flight. Males typically perch on sunlit leaves of shrubs or small trees (often on their hosts) and readily interact with other individuals, often spiraling high into the air before returning to a nearby perch. Unlike most other butterflies, female Red-banded Hairstreaks do not lay eggs directly on the larval host. Instead, they land on the ground below appropriate hosts and deposit the small eggs singly on underside of dead, fallen leaves or other debris. The resulting young larvae must crawl a considerable distance up the trunk of the plant in order to reach growing leaves.

Red-banded Hairstreak
Calycopis cecrops

Family/Subfamily: Gossamer Wings (Lycaenidae)/ Hairstreaks (Theclinae)

Wingspan: 0.75–1.00" (1.9–2.5 cm)

Above: male is slate gray above with no markings; female is slate gray with iridescent blue on hindwing; hindwing bears two short tails

Below: light gray with broad, red hindwing band outlined on one side by a thin, wavy white line; blue scaling and a black eyespot near tails

Sexes: similar, although female has metallic blue scaling above

Egg: cream brown, laid on dead leaves below host

Larva: pinkish brown with numerous short hairs

Larval Host Plants: feeds on dead plant material; associated with various trees including Wax Myrtle, Winged Sumac and Mango

Habitat: woodland edges and adjacent disturbed, brushy areas, suburban gardens

Broods: multiple generations

Abundance: common

Compare: Southern Hairstreak (pg. 91) lacks complete red hindwing band.

Resident

Jan. Feb. Mar. Apr. May June July Aug. Sept. Oct. Nov. Dec.

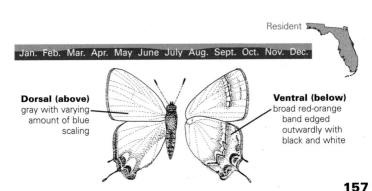

Dorsal (above)
gray with varying amount of blue scaling

Ventral (below)
broad red-orange band edged outwardly with black and white

157

Larva

Comments: The boldly marked Bartram's Hairstreak is primarily restricted to the remaining pine rockland habitat within Everglades National Park and Key Deer National Wildlife Refuge on Big Pine Key. With specialized habitat requirements and a restricted range, the butterfly has periodically been the subject of debate for potential listing on state and federal endangered species lists. Adults have a quick, darting flight but never wander far from their larval hosts and even utilize Wooly Croton as a nectar source. The butterfly can be found during every month of the year in south Florida.

Bartram's Hairstreak
Strymon acis bartrami

Family/Subfamily: Gossamer Wings (Lycaenidae)/ Hairstreaks (Theclinae)

Wingspan: 0.9–1.1" (2.3–2.8 cm)

Above: slate gray with bright reddish orange-capped black hindwing eyespot above tails

Below: light gray; hindwing has two white spots at base and two white lines intersecting in a reddish orange submarginal patch near long tails

Sexes: similar

Egg: cream, laid singly on host flowers

Larva: light olive green with numerous short hairs

Larval Host Plants: Woolly Croton

Habitat: pine rocklands

Broods: multiple generations

Abundance: occasional and very localized; of conservation concern

Compare: Gray Hairstreak (pg. 161) and Martial's Hairstreak (*Strymon martialis*) lack broad white ventral hindwing bands and basal white spots.

Resident

Jan. Feb. Mar. Apr. May June July Aug. Sept. Oct. Nov. Dec.

Dorsal (above)
orange-capped black spot
long tails

Ventral (below)
two white spots
thick white line
large orange patch

159

Ventral

Larva

Comments: Widespread and abundant, the Gray Hairstreak is one of the most commonly encountered hairstreaks in Florida. It is extremely fond of flowers and a frequent garden visitor. The small hairlike tails on the hindwing resemble antennae and help deflect the attack of would-be predators away from the insect's vulnerable body. This charade, employed by many members of the family, is enhanced by the bright orange eyespots and converging lines on the wings below that draw attention to the unique feature.

Gray Hairstreak
Strymon melinus

Family/Subfamily: Gossamer Wings (Lycaenidae)/ Hairstreaks (Theclinae)

Wingspan: 1.0–1.5" (2.5–3.8 cm)

Above: slate gray with distinct reddish orange-capped black hindwing spot above tail

Below: light gray with black-and-white line across both wings (often with some orange); hindwing has reddish orange-capped black spot and blue scaling above tail

Sexes: similar; female larger with broader wings

Egg: light green, laid singly on flower buds or flowers of host

Larva: highly variable; bright green with lateral cream stripes to pinkish red

Larval Host Plants: wide variety of plants including Partridge Pea, beggarweeds, milk peas, White Clover and Sida

Habitat: open, disturbed sites including roadsides, fallow agricultural land, old fields and gardens

Broods: multiple generations

Abundance: common

Compare: White M Hairstreak (pg. 73) has orange ventral hindwing spot without black pupil and distinct zigzag white line.

Resident

Jan. Feb. Mar. Apr. May June July Aug. Sept. Oct. Nov. Dec.

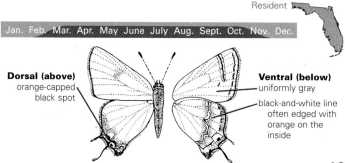

Dorsal (above)
orange-capped black spot

Ventral (below)
uniformly gray

black-and-white line often edged with orange on the inside

Larva

Comments: This attractive Florida endemic occurs in small, highly localized and geographically isolated colonies throughout coastal and interior counties of north-central Florida. Unlike many other species, the butterfly spends the majority of its adult life directly on the host trees, leaving only occasionally to nectar at nearby blossoms or possibly disperse to locate or establish new colony sites. The species was historically aided by the planting of native cedar trees along roads for windbreaks or home landscaping. Presently though, it faces an uphill battle for survival as more of its critical habitat is lost or altered by development.

Sweadner's Hairstreak
Callophrys swaedneri

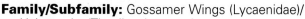

Family/Subfamily: Gossamer Wings (Lycaenidae)/ Hairstreaks (Theclinae)

Wingspan: 0.8–1.1" (2.0–2.8 cm)

Above: brown with amber scaling and dark borders

Below: olive green; hindwing has two small white spots near wing base and irregular white postmedian line edged on inside with reddish brown; blue scaling and black submarginal spots near tail

Sexes: similar

Egg: light green, laid singly on host

Larva: bright green with numerous white markings on back and sides

Larval Host Plants: Southern Red Cedar

Habitat: dry fields, forest edges and coastal areas containing Southern Red Cedar

Broods: multiple generations

Abundance: uncommon and very localized; of conservation concern

Compare: Olive Hairstreak (*Callophrys gryneus*) is extremely similar but is not found in north central Florida. Individuals encountered elsewhere have larger white postbasal bars on the underside of the hindwing and reddish brown scaling in black submarginal spot near the tails.

Resident

Jan. Feb. Mar. Apr. May June July Aug. Sept. Oct. Nov. Dec.

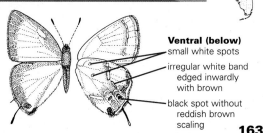

Dorsal (above)

Ventral (below)
small white spots

irregular white band edged inwardly with brown

black spot without reddish brown scaling

163

Ventral Larva

Comments: Named for the mineral of the same color, the Malachite is considered by many to be the most beautiful butterfly in Florida. A relatively recent colonist to the state, it was a rare find prior to 1965. Now, it is locally common throughout the extreme southern counties. The butterfly is found along the weedy edges of tropical hammocks and within overgrown commercial nurseries and fruit groves. It is a large butterfly with a fast, powerful flight. Adults prefer rotting fruit instead of flower nectar. It is the only large butterfly in Florida with green markings.

Malachite
Siproeta stelenes

Family/Subfamily: Brush-foots (Nymphalidae)/
True Brush-foots (Nymphalinae)

Wingspan: 2.8–3.3" (7.1–8.4 cm)

Above: brown with large green patches and spots; hindwing bears a short, stubby tail

Below: similar to above with brownish orange wings and
green patches

Sexes: similar

Egg: small green eggs laid singly on host leaves

Larva: velvety black with numerous reddish orange
branched spines

Larval Host Plants: Green Shrimp Plant

Habitat: hammock edges and adjacent disturbed sites

Broods: multiple generations

Abundance: occasional; localized

Compare: unique

Resident Stray

| Jan. | Feb. | Mar. | Apr. | May | June | July | Aug. | Sept. | Oct. | Nov. | Dec. |

male

Dorsal (above)
big translucent
green spots

tail

Ventral (below)
brownish orange

Comments: Easily overlooked, the Southern Skipperling is Florida's smallest skipper. It occasionally visits home gardens. Adults have a weak, darting flight and skim quickly over low vegetation stopping now and then to perch on available leaves or grass blades. The butterfly may be encountered year-round in Florida.

Southern Skipperling
Copaeodes minima

Family/Subfamily: Skippers (Hesperiidae)/
Banded Skippers (Hesperiinae)

Wingspan: 0.50–0.75" (1.3–1.9 cm)

Above: elongated wings; male is bright tawny orange;
female is brownish orange with darker scaling toward
wing bases and along margins

Below: yellow orange with narrow, cream streak through
hindwing

Sexes: similar, although female somewhat darker

Egg: laid singly on host leaves

Larva: green

Larval Host Plants: Bermuda Grass and possibly others

Habitat: open, grassy areas including roadsides, utility
easements, old fields, meadows and forest edges

Broods: multiple generations

Abundance: occasional to common; local

Compare: Least Skipper (pg. 171) is larger, has more
rounded wings with dark dorsal borders and lacks
whitish ventral hindwing streak

Resident

Jan. Feb. Mar. Apr. May June July Aug. Sept. Oct. Nov. Dec.

Dorsal (above)
elongated wings

Ventral (below)
all yellow orange

cream streak

167

Ventral

Comments: A representative of a subfamily that reaches tremendous diversity in the neotropics, this is Florida's only metalmark species. It scurries among the vegetation with a low, quick flight. Adults regularly perch on flowers or leaves with their wings spread. Although spotty and localized throughout the state, it is often abundant when encountered.

Little Metalmark
Calephelis virginiensis

Family/Subfamily: Gossamer Wings (Lycaenidae)/ Metalmarks (Riodininae)

Wingspan: 0.5–1.0" (1.3–2.5 cm)

Above: brownish orange with numerous delicate dark markings and two narrow, metallic gray bands along the outer edge of the wings

Below: similar to upper surface; brownish orange with dark spots and metallic gray bands

Sexes: similar, although female has broader, more rounded wings

Egg: laid singly on host leaves

Larva: pale green with long white hairs

Larval Host Plants: Yellow Thistle

Habitat: open grassy areas, pine savannahs, moist meadows and forest edges

Broods: multiple generations

Abundance: occasional, locally abundant

Compare: unique

Resident

Jan. Feb. Mar. Apr. May June July Aug. Sept. Oct. Nov. Dec.

Dorsal (above)
dark fringe
dark reticulation
metallic bands

Ventral (below)
metallic bands

Ventral

Comments: The Least Skipper has a low, weak flight and flutters slowly through the vegetation, occasionally pausing to nectar or perch. They regularly visit flowers but prefer low plants with small blossoms. It is not a regular garden visitor.

Least Skipper
Ancyloxypha numitor

Family/Subfamily: Skippers (Hesperiidae)/
Banded Skippers (Hesperiinae)

Wingspan: 0.7–1.0" (1.8–2.5 cm)

Above: forewing orange-brown with dark border; hind-wing orange with dark border

Below: forewing black with orange border; hindwing orange-gold

Sexes: similar

Egg: yellow, laid singly on or near host leaves

Larva: long and slender, light yellow-green with thin dark dorsal stripe and reddish brown head; head has numerous cream stripes

Larval Host Plants: various grasses

Habitat: moist, grassy areas including roadside ditches, utility easements, wet meadows, pond edges and old fields

Broods: multiple generations

Abundance: occasional to common

Compare: The Southern Skipperling (pg. 167) is smaller and has distinct light ray on the hindwing below.

Resident

Jan. Feb. Mar. Apr. May June July Aug. Sept. Oct. Nov. Dec.

male

Dorsal (above)
orange
heavy dark margin

Ventral (below)
black

171

Male

Male ventral

Female

Female ventral

Larva

Comments: The lovely tawny-orange Pearl Crescent is our most widespread and abundant crescent. It is seasonally variable, and spring and fall individuals are darker and more heavily patterned on the ventral hindwings. It is an opportunistic breeder, continually producing new generations as long as favorable conditions allow. It has a rapid, erratic flight. Males perch on low vegetation with wings outstretched and frequently patrol for females. Freshly emerged males often gather at moist ground.

Pearl Crescent
Phyciodes tharos

Family/Subfamily: Brush-foots (Nymphalidae)/
True Brush-foots (Nymphalinae)

Wingspan: 0.9–1.2" (2.3–3.0 cm)

Above: orange with dark bands, spots and wing borders

Below: seasonally variable; light brownish orange with
brown markings; winter-form has increased dark coloration and pattern elements

Sexes: similar, although female has increased black
markings

Egg: green, laid in clusters on the underside of host
leaves

Larva: dark brown to charcoal with lateral cream stripes
and numerous short, branched spines

Larval Host Plants: various asters including Frost
Aster and Bushy Aster

Habitat: open, sunny locations including roadsides, old
fields, utility easements, forest edges and gardens

Broods: multiple generations

Abundance: occasional to common

Compare: Phaon Crescent (pg. 175) has yellow-orange
postmedian forewing band and lighter ventral hindwing
coloration.

Resident

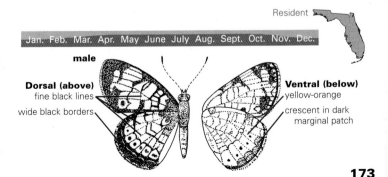

Jan. Feb. Mar. Apr. May June July Aug. Sept. Oct. Nov. Dec.

male

Dorsal (above)
fine black lines
wide black borders

Ventral (below)
yellow-orange
crescent in dark
marginal patch

173

Male

Male ventral

Comments: The Phaon Crescent remains close to its low-growing host. Adults have a low, rapid flight and are easily disturbed. Males perch on low vegetation and frequently patrol for females. They occasionally gather at moist ground. The larvae are gregarious when young but become solitary towards maturity.

Phaon Crescent
Phyciodes phaon

Family/Subfamily: Brush-foots (Nymphalidae)/
True Brush-foots (Nymphalinae)

Wingspan: 0.90–1.25" (2.3–3.2 cm)

Above: orange with dark spots, bands and wing borders;
forewing has pale yellow orange postmedian band

Below: seasonally variable; cream with brown bands,
spots and patches; winter-form has increased brown
coloration on ventral hindwings

Sexes: similar

Egg: light green, laid in clusters on the underside of host
leaves

Larva: amber brown with dark brown lines and short,
branched spines

Larval Host Plants: Frogfruit

Habitat: open, disturbed sites including roadsides, old
fields, moist ditches, utility easements, fallow agricultural land and pond edges

Broods: multiple generations

Abundance: occasional to common; locally abundant

Compare: Pearl Crescent (pg. 173) is tawny orange
below and lacks dorsal cream postmedian forewing
band.

Resident

Jan. Feb. Mar. Apr. May June July Aug. Sept. Oct. Nov. Dec.

Dorsal (above)
pale median band

extensive black
markings and
borders

Ventral (below)
tan with fine brown
lines

pale crescent in dark
marginal patch

Male

Female   Larva

Comments: The Fiery Skipper has a rapid, darting flight
but frequently stops to perch on low vegetation.
Adults are exceedingly fond of flowers and readily congregate at available blossoms. They have a strong
preference for colorful composites. The larvae utilize a
variety of grasses including many commonly planted
for lawns. As a result, the butterfly is often mentioned
as a minor turf pest. It is often found alongside the
similar-looking and equally abundant Sachem and
Whirlabout.

Fiery Skipper
Hylephila phyleus

Family/Subfamily: Skippers (Hesperiidae)/
Banded Skippers (Hesperiinae)

Wingspan: 1.00–1.25" (2.5–3.2 cm)

Above: elongated wings; male is golden orange with
jagged black border and black stigma; female is dark
brown with tawny orange spots

Below: hindwing golden orange in male or light brown in
female with tiny dark brown spots

Sexes: dissimilar; female darker with reduced orange
markings

Egg: whitish green, laid singly on host leaves

Larva: greenish brown with thin, dark brown dorsal
stripe and black head

Larval Host Plants: a wide variety of grasses including
Bermuda Grass and St. Augustine Grass

Habitat: open, grassy areas including old fields, roadsides, vacant lots, open woodlands, forest edges,
parks, lawns and gardens

Broods: multiple generations

Abundance: common to abundant

Compare: Whirlabout (pg. 179) is similar in size and
color but has noticeably larger dark spots on the ventral hindwing.

Resident

Jan. Feb. Mar. Apr. May June July Aug. Sept. Oct. Nov. Dec.

male

Dorsal (above)
jagged black
margins

Ventral (below)
small scattered spots

Male

Female pg. 85

Comments: The Whirlabout is a diminutive skipper with two distinct rows of squarish spots on the hindwings below. This species is sexually dimorphic. Males are tawny orange and considerably brighter than their drab brown female counterparts. It regularly expands its range each summer, establishing temporary breeding colonies throughout the southeast from Maryland to Texas. Living up to its name, adults have a low, erratic flight and scurry quickly around, periodically stopping to perch or nectar. Avidly fond of flowers, the butterfly is a frequent garden visitor.

Whirlabout
Polites vibex

Family/Subfamily: Skippers (Hesperiidae)/
Banded Skippers (Hesperiinae)

Wingspan: 1.00–1.25" (2.5–3.2 cm)

Above: elongated wings; golden orange with black borders and black stigma; female is dark brown with
cream spots on forewing

Below: hindwing yellow in male or bronze brown in
female with two loose bands of large dark brown
spots

Sexes: dissimilar; female brown above with little orange
scaling; olive brown below with similar pattern as male

Egg: white, laid singly on host leaves

Larva: brownish green with thin, dark dorsal stripe and
black head

Larval Host Plants: various grasses including Bermuda
Grass, St. Augustine Grass and Crabgrass

Habitat: open, disturbed areas including old fields, roadsides, vacant lots, open woodlands, forest edges,
parks, lawns and gardens

Broods: multiple generations

Abundance: common to abundant

Compare: Fiery Skipper (pg. 177) is similar in size and
color but has scattered, tiny dark spots on ventral hindwing.

Resident

Jan. Feb. Mar. Apr. May June July Aug. Sept. Oct. Nov. Dec.

male

Dorsal (above)
orange

large black stigma

jagged black
border

Ventral (below)
large black spots

golden yellow

Comments: Unique in appearance, the Harvester tends to be very localized and is seldom encountered in large numbers. Freshly emerged males often drink from moist ground along forest trails or roadsides. The butterfly has a fast, erratic flight and can be a challenge to follow. Adults feed primarily on aphid honeydew. The Harvester is the only North American butterfly with predaceous larvae.

Harvester
Feniseca tarquinius

Family/Subfamily: Gossamer Wings (Lycaenidae)/ Harvesters (Miletinae)

Wingspan: 1.1–1.3" (2.8–3.3 cm)

Above: orange with dark spots, patches and borders

Below: brown; forewing has orange central scaling and several dark patches outlined in white; hindwing has numerous dark spots outlined in white and silver scaling toward base

Sexes: similar

Egg: greenish white, laid singly among aphid colonies

Larva: gray with whitish yellow bumps bordered with brown along top, reddish brown lateral stripes and long gray hairs

Larval Host Plants: carnivorous on woolly aphids

Habitat: forest edges, moist woodlands and associated clearings, trails, waterways and roads

Broods: multiple generations

Abundance: occasional

Compare: unique

Resident

Jan. Feb. Mar. Apr. May June July Aug. Sept. Oct. Nov. Dec.

female

Dorsal (above)
orange with black markings and spots

Ventral (below)
reddish brown with silver scaling and numerous brown spots outlined in white

181

Female

Male

Comments: The Delaware Skipper is a small orange butterfly with elongated, somewhat pointed forewings. The ventral wing surface is immaculate golden yellow. Found primarily in a variety of moist, grassy habitats from damp meadows to coastal marshes, the butterfly frequently finds its way into suburban yards. Adults have a quick, darting flight and are fond of flowers. Males perch on low leaves and grasses and make frequent exploratory flights.

Delaware Skipper
Anatrytone logan

Family/Subfamily: Skippers (Hesperiidae)/
Banded Skippers (Hesperiinae)

Wingspan: 1.0–1.4" (2.5–3.6 cm)

Above: brownish orange; forewings are elongated and
somewhat pointed; male has dark borders and veins
and a small black cell-end bar on forewing; female has
dark veins and wide borders, forewing cell has a large
brown bar

Below: golden orange with brown bar along trailing edge
of forewing; hindwing unmarked

Sexes: similar, although female darker with reduced
orange coloration

Egg: white, laid singly on host leaves

Larva: bluish white with dark tubercles and a black-and-
white head

Larval Host Plants: various grasses including
bluestems and Switch Grass

Habitat: open woodlands, forest edges, roadsides, pastures, wetland edges and old fields

Broods: two generations

Abundance: occasional

Compare: Least Skipper (pg. 171) is smaller, has more
rounded wings and dark brown ventral forewing with
gold border.

Resident

Jan. Feb. Mar. Apr. May June July Aug. Sept. Oct. Nov. Dec.

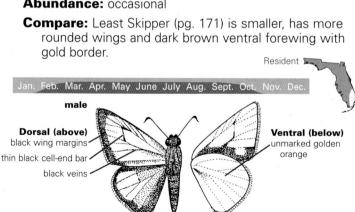

male

Dorsal (above)
black wing margins
thin black cell-end bar
black veins

Ventral (below)
unmarked golden
orange

Male

Female pg. 95   Male   Female

Comments: The Sachem shares its affinity for open, disturbed sites with the Whirlabout and Fiery Skipper with which it often flies. Adults have a quick, darting flight that is usually low to the ground. All three species are somewhat nervous butterflies, but readily congregate at available flowers. Together, they often form a circus of activity with several pausing briefly to perch or nectar before one flies up and disturbs the others, only to alight again moments later.

Sachem
Atalopedes campestris

Family/Subfamily: Skippers (Hesperiidae)/
Banded Skippers (Hesperiinae)

Wingspan: 1.0–1.5" (2.5–3.8 cm)

Above: elongated wings; male is golden orange with
brown borders and large, black stigma; female is dark
brown with golden markings in wing centers; forewing
has black median spot and several semitransparent
spots

Below: variable; hindwing golden brown in male, brown
in female with pale postmedian patch or band of spots

Sexes: dissimilar; female darker with reduced orange
markings

Egg: white, laid singly on host leaves

Larva: greenish brown with thin, dark dorsal stripe and
black head

Larval Host Plants: various grasses including Bermuda
Grass and Crabgrass

Habitat: open, disturbed areas including old fields, pastures, roadsides, parks, lawns and gardens

Broods: multiple generations

Abundance: common to abundant

Compare: Fiery Skipper (pg. 177) and Whirlabout (pg.
179) have dark spots on the ventral hindwing.

Resident

Jan. Feb. Mar. Apr. May June July Aug. Sept. Oct. Nov. Dec.

male

Dorsal (above)
large squarish stigma
golden orange

Ventral (below)
large pale patch or
postmedian band

Comments: The Palatka Skipper, also called the Sawgrass Skipper, is generally found in close proximity to its larval host. Adults have a strong, rapid flight and frequently visit available flowers. Males perch on low vegetation and readily investigate passing objects. The larvae construct individual shelters on the host by tying leaves together with silk.

Palatka Skipper
Euphyes palatka

Family/Subfamily: Skippers (Hesperiidae)/
Banded Skippers (Hesperiinae)

Wingspan: 1.40–1.75" (3.6–4.4 cm)

Above: male is tawny orange with dark brown borders
and narrow black forewing stigma; female is brown
with reduced orange

Below: rust; forewing dark brown toward base and along
trailing edge

Sexes: similar, female has muted and reduced orange
markings

Egg: light green, laid singly on host leaves

Larva: green with fine black dots; head is whitish with
three black stripes

Larval Host Plants: Sawgrass

Habitat: wetlands, marshes

Broods: multiple generations

Abundance: occasional

Compare: Palmetto Skipper (*Euphyes arpa*) is similar in
size but has golden orange wings below, and head and
thorax are golden orange.

Resident

| Jan. | Feb. | Mar. | Apr. | May | June | July | Aug. | Sept. | Oct. | Nov. | Dec. |

male

Dorsal (above)
thick dark border

Ventral (below)
dull reddish brown

Male

Female **Winter** **Larva**

Comments: Much debate centers on the origin of the
butterfly's common name. One interpretation points to
its narrow black forewing spot, which to many
observers resembles a closed eye. Nonetheless, the
Sleepy Orange is far from lethargic. Adults are
extremely active and have a quick, nervous flight.
Another of Florida's migratory species, individuals produced late in the season move south and overwinter
in reproductive diapause. Newly emerged males often
gather in large numbers at mud puddles or damp
ground.

Sleepy Orange
Eurema nicippe

Family/Subfamily: Whites and Sulphurs (Pieridae)/ Sulphurs (Coliadinae)

Wingspan: 1.3–2.0" (3.3–5.1 cm)

Above: bright orange with broad irregular black wing borders; forewing cell bears small, elongated black spot

Below: hindwings seasonally variable; butter-yellow with brown markings in summer-form and tan to reddish brown with darker pattern elements in winter-form

Sexes: similar, although females larger and less vibrant with heavier hindwing pattern

Egg: white, laid singly on host leaves

Larva: green with thin, cream lateral stripe and numerous short hairs

Larval Host Plants: various cassia species including Sicklepod Senna, Christmas Senna and Coffee Senna

Habitat: open, disturbed sites including roadsides, utility easements, vacant fields, agricultural land, parks and home gardens

Broods: multiple generations; adults may be found year-round; particularly numerous in late summer and fall

Abundance: common

Compare: Orange Sulphur (pg. 191) has dorsal orange hindwing spot and distinct, red-rimmed ventral hindwing silver spot.

Resident

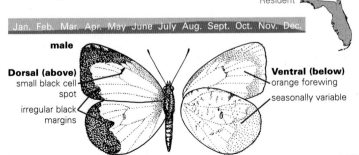

Jan. Feb. Mar. Apr. May June July Aug. Sept. Oct. Nov. Dec.

male

Dorsal (above)
small black cell spot

irregular black margins

Ventral (below)
orange forewing

seasonally variable

189

Larva

Comments: Although common and widespread throughout much of North America, the Orange Sulphur is
infrequently encountered in Florida. It has a low, rapid
flight. Fond of open, weedy sites, the species is particularly abundant in and around cultivated alfalfa fields,
where it occasionally can become a serious pest.
Males often gather at moist ground or gravel.

Orange Sulphur
Colias eurytheme

Family/Subfamily: Whites and Sulphurs (Pieridae)/ Sulphurs (Coliadinae)

Wingspan: 1.6–2.4" (4.1–6.1 cm)

Above: bright yellow orange with black wing borders and black forewing cell spot; hindwing has central orange spot

Below: yellow with row of dark submarginal spots; hind-wing has one or two central red-rimmed silvery spots

Sexes: similar, although female has yellow spots in black wing borders and are less vibrant; female rarely white

Egg: white, laid singly on host leaves

Larva: green with thin, cream lateral stripe and numerous short hairs

Larval Host Plants: Alfalfa, White Sweet Clover and White Clover

Habitat: open, sunny sites including roadsides, vacant fields, agricultural land, parks and home gardens

Broods: multiple generations

Abundance: uncommon to occasional

Compare: Southern Dogface (pg. 243) is larger, has pointed forewings and wide, scalloped forewing borders.

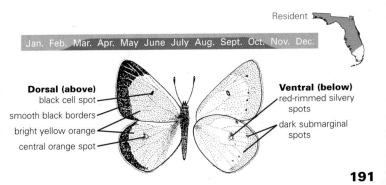

Resident

Jan. Feb. Mar. Apr. May June July Aug. Sept. Oct. Nov. Dec.

Dorsal (above)
black cell spot
smooth black borders
bright yellow orange
central orange spot

Ventral (below)
red-rimmed silvery spots
dark submarginal spots

Ventral

Larva

Comments: The medium-sized Variegated Fritillary shares its affinity for open, sunny habitats with the similar-looking Gulf Fritillary but is generally less common and highly local in occurrence. Adults have low, erratic flight but regularly stop to nectar at available flowers. It is an occasional garden visitor.

Variegated Fritillary
Euptoieta claudia

Family/Subfamily: Brush-foots (Nymphalidae)/ Longwing Butterflies (Heliconiinae)

Wingspan: 1.75–2.25" (4.4–5.7 cm)

Above: brownish orange with dark markings and narrow light median band

Below: overall brown; forewing has basal orange scaling; hindwing mottled with tan, cream and dark brown

Sexes: similar, although female is larger and has broader wings

Egg: tiny cream eggs laid singly on host leaves and tendrils

Larva: orange with black-spotted white stripes and black spines

Larval Host Plants: various violets and Passion Flower vines

Habitat: open, sunny sites including roadsides, pastures, old fields and utility easements

Broods: multiple generations

Abundance: occasional to locally abundant

Compare: Gulf Fritillary (pg. 207) brighter orange with silvery ventral spots. Julia (pg. 215) has elongated, narrow orange wings with few black markings.

Resident

Jan. Feb. Mar. Apr. May June July Aug. Sept. Oct. Nov. Dec.

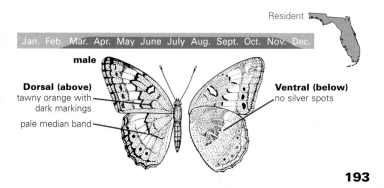

male

Dorsal (above)
tawny orange with dark markings
pale median band

Ventral (below)
no silver spots

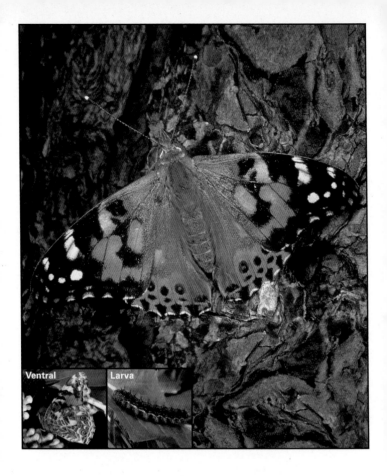

Ventral   Larva

Comments: The Painted Lady, a resident of northern
Mexico, annually colonizes much of North America
each year before migrating south again in the fall.
Although abundance varies from year to year, it is
infrequently encountered in Florida. It is a butterfly of
open disturbed sites, but may be found in most habitats when dispersing. The larvae construct individual
shelters of loose webbing on host leaves.

Painted Lady
Vanessa cardui

Family/Subfamily: Brush-foots (Nymphalidae)/ True Brush-foots (Nymphalinae)

Wingspan: 1.75–2.40" (4.4–6.1 cm)

Above: pinkish orange with dark markings and small white spots near tip of forewing

Below: brown with cream patches in ornate cobweb pattern; hindwing has row of four small eyespots and marginal band of lavender spots

Sexes: similar

Egg: small pale green eggs laid singly on host leaves

Larva: variable; greenish yellow with black mottling to charcoal with cream mottling and several rows of light-colored, branched spines

Larval Host Plants: large variety of plants including thistles and mallows

Habitat: open, disturbed sites including roadsides, old fields, fallow agricultural land, pastures, utility easements and gardens

Broods: multiple generations

Abundance: rare to occasional

Compare: American Painted Lady (pg. 197) similar in size and color but has two large ventral hindwing eyespots.

Resident

Jan. Feb. Mar. Apr. May June July Aug. Sept. Oct. Nov. Dec.

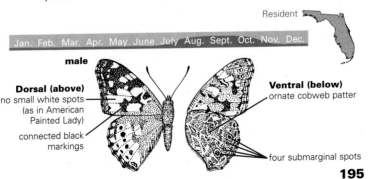

male

Dorsal (above)
no small white spots (as in American Painted Lady)

connected black markings

Ventral (below)
ornate cobweb patter

four submarginal spots

195

Ventral

Larva

Comments: Considered a common butterfly, the American Painted Lady is often overlooked despite its attractiveness. The intricately detailed, agate-like design on the underside of the wings is a sharp contrast to the bold orange and black pattern above. Nervous and wary, it is difficult to approach and a challenge to closely observe. When disturbed, it takes off in a low, erratic flight but often returns to a nearby location just a few moments later. The larvae construct individual shelters on the host by spinning together leaves and flowerheads with silk. Inside, the larvae safely rest when not actively feeding.

American Painted Lady
Vanessa virginiensis

Family/Subfamily: Brush-foots (Nymphalidae)/
True Brush-foots (Nymphalinae)

Wingspan: 1.75–2.40" (4.4–6.1 cm)

Above: orange with dark markings and borders; forewing
has small white spots near apex

Below: brown with ornate, cream cobweb pattern; hindwing has two large eyespots and narrow lavender
marginal band

Sexes: similar; females with broader wings

Egg: small pale green eggs laid singly on upper surface
of host leaves

Larva: variable; greenish yellow with narrow black bands
to black with cream bands and numerous red-based,
branched spines; pair of prominent white spots on
each segment

Larval Host Plants: Purple Cudweed, Wandering
Cudweed, Narrow-leaved Cudweed, Sweet Everlasting
and others

Habitat: open, disturbed sites including roadsides, old
fields, pastures, utility easements and gardens

Broods: multiple generations; adults overwinter

Abundance: common to abundant

Compare: Painted Lady (pg. 195) has a row of four small
ventral hindwing eyespots.

Resident

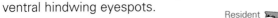
Jan. Feb. Mar. Apr. May June July Aug. Sept. Oct. Nov. Dec.

Dorsal (above)
small white spot
disconnected black markings
some blue in one or more eyespots

Ventral (below)
small white spot
ornate cobweb pattern
two large eyespots

197

Male

Female pg. 141 | Male | Female

Comments: Sexually dimorphic, the Zabulon Skipper is a small butterfly with a bright orange male and a drab brown female. It occasionally wanders into suburban gardens. Adults have a rapid flight and are strongly attracted to flowers. Males perch on sunlit branches along trails or clearings and engage passing objects or rival males. Females generally prefer to remain within the confines of nearby shady sites.

Zabulon Skipper
Poanes zabulon

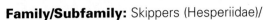

Family/Subfamily: Skippers (Hesperiidae)/
Banded Skippers (Hesperiinae)

Wingspan: 1.0–1.4" (2.5–3.6 cm)

Above: male is golden orange with dark brown borders
and small brown spot near forewing apex; female is
dark brown with band of cream spots across forewing

Below: male hindwing yellow with brown base and margin enclosing a yellow spot; female is dark brown with
small band of light spots near forewing apex, lavender
scaling on wing margins, and white band along apex

Sexes: dissimilar, female brown with little orange color

Egg: pale green, laid singly on host leaves

Larva: tan with dark dorsal stripe, white lateral stripe and
reddish brown head; body is covered with short, light-
colored hairs

Larval Host Plants: various grasses including
Purpletop Grass and lovegrass

Habitat: open woodlands, forest edges, roadsides, pastures, wetland edges, stream corridors and old fields

Broods: two generations

Abundance: occasional

Compare: Sachem (pg. 185) is similar to male Zabulon
Skipper, but dark hindwing base does not enclose yellow patch.

Resident

Jan. Feb. Mar. Apr. May June July Aug. Sept. Oct. Nov. Dec.

male

Dorsal (above)
dark spot

golden orange

Ventral (below)
dark base encloses
yellow spot

yellow with spots

Male

Female

Comments: The Large Orange Sulphur is an abundant butterfly throughout the Keys and coastal portions of the mainland. Adults have a strong, directed flight but are fond of flowers and regularly stop to nectar. Males occasionally visit moist ground. It is restricted to south Florida and rarely disperses northward.

Large Orange Sulphur
Phoebis agarithe

Family/Subfamily: Whites and Sulphurs (Pieridae)/ Sulphurs (Coliadinae)

Wingspan: 2.2–3.0" (5.6–7.6 cm)

Above: male is bright orange with no pattern elements; female is pale orange to near white with dark-spotted forewing border, black cell spot and dark diagonal forewing line; seasonally variable

Below: diagonal forewing line; male is bright orange-yellow with faint reddish brown spots; female is pale yellow with pinkish brown markings and two silver spots in middle of hindwing; seasonally variable; winter-form darker and more heavily marked

Sexes: dissimilar; female lighter with increased pattern

Egg: yellow, laid singly on new growth of host

Larva: green with thin, cream-yellow lateral stripe

Larval Host Plants: Wild Tamarind, Blackbead and Cat's Claw

Habitat: tropical hammocks and adjacent open area

Broods: multiple generations

Abundance: occasional to common

Compare: Cloudless Sulphur (pg. 245) is yellow and lacks diagonal forewing line. Orange-barred Sulphur (pg. 247) is yellow to white with orange forewing bars or broken diagonal forewing bar.

Resident

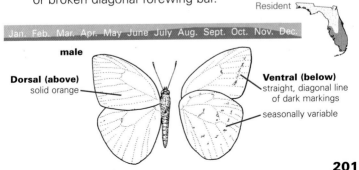

Jan. Feb. Mar. Apr. May June July Aug. Sept. Oct. Nov. Dec.

male

Dorsal (above)
solid orange

Ventral (below)
straight, diagonal line of dark markings

seasonally variable

201

Ventral Winter Larva

Comments: The Question Mark's dark markings, irregular wing edges and cryptically colored undersides help the butterfly resemble a dead leaf when resting. Adults have a strong, rapid flight but frequently alight on overhanging branches, tree trunks or leaf litter. Wary and nervous, they are often difficult to closely approach. Males readily establish territories and aggressively investigate any passing objects. Both sexes visit rotting fruit, dung, carrion and tree sap.

Question Mark
Polygonia interrogationis

Family/Subfamily: Brush-foots (Nymphalidae)/
True Brush-foots (Nymphalinae)

Wingspan: 2.25–3.00" (5.7–7.6 cm)

Above: seasonally variable; dark brown with orange coloration and dark spots on forewing; narrow lavender borders and irregular, jagged edges; winter-form has increased orange on hindwing and longer tails

Below: seasonally variable; pinkish brown dead leaf appearance; hindwing has two, small median silvery spots that form a question mark

Sexes: similar

Egg: green, laid singly or in small groups on top of each other on host leaves

Larva: gray to black with orange and cream stripes and spots and several rows of branched spines

Larval Host Plants: Sugarberry, American Elm, Winged Elm

Habitat: deciduous forests, moist woodlands, forest edges and adjacent open areas

Broods: multiple generations

Abundance: occasional

Compare: Goatweed Butterfly (pg. 205) has pointed forewing apex and lacks white question mark on hindwing.

Resident

Jan. Feb. Mar. Apr. May June July Aug. Sept. Oct. Nov. Dec.

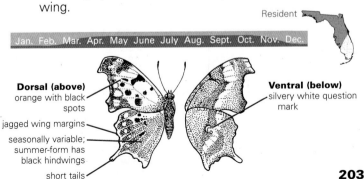

Dorsal (above)
orange with black spots

jagged wing margins

seasonally variable; summer-form has black hindwings

short tails

Ventral (below)
silvery white question mark

203

Male

Ventral   Winter   Larva

Comments: Named after its larval host, the Goatweed Butterfly has a leaf-like pattern on the wings below. Rarely encountered in large numbers, adults have a strong, rapid flight. Adults perch with their wings closed on the trunks of trees, branches or on the ground and can be quite a challenge to find, let alone closely approach. The butterfly prefers rotting fruit and sap over flower nectar. It produces distinct seasonal forms.

Goatweed Butterfly
Anaea andria

Family/Subfamily: Brush-foots (Nymphalidae)/
Leafwings (Charaxinae)

Wingspan: 2.25–3.00" (5.7–7.6 cm)

Above: pointed forewings and hindwing tail; male is
bright reddish orange; female is lighter orange with
dark markings and pale band along wing margins

Below: seasonally variable; brownish gray resembling a
dead leaf; winter-form is more heavily patterned, has
longer hindwing tails and a more pronounced forewing
point

Sexes: similar, although female is lighter with more
extensive markings

Egg: gray-green, laid singly on host leaves

Larva: gray-green with light head and numerous tiny light
spots

Larval Host Plants: Silver Croton

Habitat: dry pinelands, woodland edges and adjacent
open areas

Broods: multiple generations; adults overwinter

Abundance: occasional; local

Compare: Question Mark (pg. 203) has irregular wing
edges and dark dorsal forewing spots.

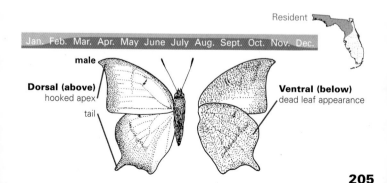

Resident

Jan. Feb. Mar. Apr. May June July Aug. Sept. Oct. Nov. Dec.

male

Dorsal (above)
hooked apex

tail

Ventral (below)
dead leaf appearance

Female

Ventral

Larva

Comments: The Gulf Fritillary's hindwings below are beautifully decorated with numerous silvery, mercury-like patches that quickly distinguish it from the equally common Monarch. It readily stops to nectar at colorful flowers and is an abundant garden visitor. Adults have a low, rapid flight. The Gulf Fritillary is one of several migratory species in the Southeast. During the fall, adults migrate southward in large numbers and over-winter in southern portions of the state.

Gulf Fritillary
Agraulis vanillae

Family/Subfamily: Brush-foots (Nymphalidae)/ Longwing Butterflies (Heliconiinae)

Wingspan: 2.5–3.0" (6.4–7.6 cm)

Above: bright orange elongated wings with black markings and three small, black-rimmed white spots on forewing cell; hindwing has chain-like black border

Below: brown with elongated silvery spots

Sexes: similar, although female is paler above with increased black markings

Egg: yellow eggs laid singly on host leaves

Larva: orange with greenish black stripes and black, branched spines

Larval Host Plants: various Passion Flower species including Maypop, Corky-Stemmed Passion Flower and Yellow Passion Flower

Habitat: open, disturbed sites including roadsides, old fields, utility easements, parks and gardens

Broods: multiple generations

Abundance: common, particularly abundant in the fall

Compare: The Gulf Fritillary's distinct ventral silver spots quickly distinguish it from the Variegated Fritillary (pg. 193), Julia (pg. 215) and Monarch (pg. 219).

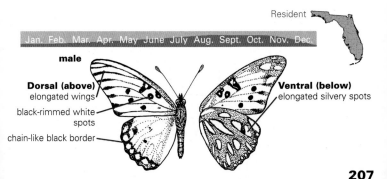

Resident

Jan. Feb. Mar. Apr. May June July Aug. Sept. Oct. Nov. Dec.

male

Dorsal (above)
elongated wings

black-rimmed white spots

chain-like black border

Ventral (below)
elongated silvery spots

207

Male

Ventral

Larva

Comments: The colorful Viceroy has a quick, gliding flight and is often wary and difficult to closely approach. Males perch on overhanging branches and occasionally dart out to explore their territory or investigate passing objects. Unlike those found throughout most of the eastern United States, the Florida subspecies is a darker, rich mahogany brown and more closely resembles the Queen. Together, the Viceroy, Queen and Monarch form a Mullerian mimicry complex in which all three species are highly distasteful or toxic to certain predators. Bright orange Viceroys can often be found in north Florida.

Viceroy
Limenitis archippus

Family/Subfamily: Brush-foots (Nymphalidae)/ Admirals and Relatives (Limenitidinae)

Wingspan: 2.6–3.20" (6.6–8.1 cm)

Above: orange to mahogany with black markings, veins and broad wing borders; borders contain central row of small, white spots; forewing has black postmedian band and white spots; hindwing has distinct thin, black postmedian line

Below: as above with lighter orange coloration and increased white markings

Sexes: similar

Egg: gray-green, laid singly on tip of host leaves

Larva: mottled green, brown and cream with two long, knobby horns on thorax

Larval Host Plants: Black Willow, Coastal Plain Willow, Weeping Willow

Habitat: pond edges, wetlands, roadside ditches and moist areas supporting willows

Broods: multiple generations

Abundance: occasional to common

Compare: Monarch (pg. 219) is larger and lacks black postmedian hindwing line. Gulf Fritillary (pg. 207) is brighter orange with elongated wings and distinct silver ventral spots.

Resident

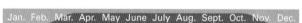

Jan. Feb. Mar. Apr. May June July Aug. Sept. Oct. Nov. Dec.

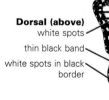

Dorsal (above)
white spots
thin black band
white spots in black border

ntral (below)
te: there is a dark orm that mimics he Queen, and a ighter orange form hat mimics the Monarch

209

Female

Ventral   Larva

Comments: Endemic to southern portions of the state, the boldly colored Florida Leafwing has a strong, powerful flight. Living up to its name, the shape, color and pattern of the wings below closely resemble a dead leaf and provide excellent camouflage from would-be predators. Found alongside Bartram's Hairstreak as both species utilize the same larval host. Sporadic in occurrence, the butterfly is often locally common but rarely seen in large numbers.

Florida Leafwing
Anaea floridalis

Family/Subfamily: Brush-foots (Nymphalidae)/ Leafwings (Charaxinae)

Wingspan: 2.75–3.20" (7.0–8.1 cm)

Above: hindwing has a short tail; male is reddish orange with faint dark markings and pointed forewings; female is reddish orange with increased dark markings and dark borders

Below: seasonally variable; grayish brown with dark markings; resembles a dead leaf; winter-form has more prominently pointed forewings, longer hindwing tails and increased dark markings

Sexes: similar, although females more extensive dark markings and wing borders

Egg: grayish green, laid singly on host leaves

Larva: grayish green with cream lateral stripe and tiny light dots; brown dorsal patch behind the thorax

Larval Host Plants: Woolly Croton

Habitat: open pinelands

Broods: multiple generations

Abundance: occasional; local; of conservation concern

Compare: Goatweed Butterfly (pg. 205) is absent from south Florida.

Resident

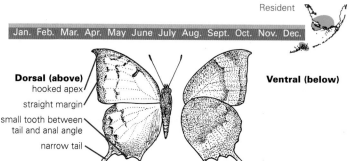

Jan. Feb. Mar. Apr. May June July Aug. Sept. Oct. Nov. Dec.

Dorsal (above)
hooked apex
straight margin
small tooth between tail and anal angle
narrow tail

Ventral (below)

Ventral

Larva

Comments: The Queen, while superficially similar in appearance to the closely related Monarch, does not undertake massive annual migrations. Adults have a slow, soaring flight and are fond of flowers. It is a frequent garden visitor and typically rests and feeds with wings closed. The larvae feed on plants in the Milkweed family and sequester various chemicals that render the butterfly highly distasteful to certain predators.

Queen
Danaus gilippus

Family/Subfamily: Brush-foots (Nymphalidae)/ Milkweed Butterflies (Danainae)

Wingspan: 3.0–3.5" (7.6–8.9 cm)

Above: mahogany with black wing borders and small white forewing spots; male has a single black post-median androconial scent patch on the hindwing

Below: reddish brown; forewing as above; hindwing has black veins and small white spots in black border

Sexes: similar; female lacks black scent patch

Egg: white, laid singly on host leaves

Larva: black with transverse cream stripes and yellow spots; body has three pairs of long, black filaments

Larval Host Plants: various milkweed family plants including Mexican Milkweed, White Swamp Milkweed, Sandhill Milkweed, White Vine and Sand Vine

Habitat: savannahs, pastures, pinelands, roadsides, old fields, utility easements, coastal areas and gardens

Broods: multiple generations

Abundance: occasional

Compare: Monarch (pg. 219) is larger, brighter orange and has black wing veins above. Gulf Fritillary (pg. 207) has elongated wings and prominent silver ventral spots.

Resident

Jan. Feb. Mar. Apr. May June July Aug. Sept. Oct. Nov. Dec.

male

Dorsal (above)
mahogany in color

white spots

veins not outlined in black

scent patch on males only

Ventral (below)
black veins on hindwing

double row of white spots

213

Ventral

Male | Female | Larva

Comments: A primarily tropical species, the Julia is a rapid flier that easily maneuvers among dense forest vegetation. Males actively patrol woodland edges, trails and adjacent open areas for females. Strongly attracted to flowers, adults readily stop at available flowers to nectar but rarely remain at any one blossom for long. They are particularly fond of Lantana and Shepherd's Needle (*Bidens alba*). Unlike most other longwing butterflies, the Julia has a relatively short lifespan, surviving only a few weeks as an adult.

Julia
Dryas iulia

Family/Subfamily: Brush-foots (Nymphalidae)/ Longwing Butterflies (Heliconiinae)

Wingspan: 3.0–3.8" (7.6–9.7 cm)

Above: wings long and narrow; orange with black sub-apical markings and narrow, black margins

Below: yellow-orange and mottled

Sexes: similar, although female is a less vibrant, duller orange and has a single black band across forewing

Egg: yellow, elongated, laid singly on new growth or tendrils of host

Larva: dark brown with branched black spines and longitudinal rows of cream spots broken by pale red markings

Larval Host Plants: various Passion Flower vines including Corky-stemmed Passion Flower and Many-flowered Passion Flower

Habitat: tropical woodlands and adjacent open areas

Broods: multiple generations; adults have been recorded from every month

Abundance: occasional

Compare: Gulf Fritillary (pg. 207) has wider wings, more black markings above and silver spotting below.

Resident Stray

Jan. Feb. Mar. Apr. May June July Aug. Sept. Oct. Nov. Dec.

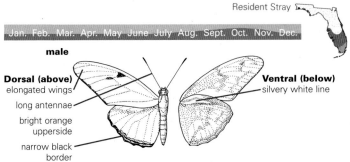

male

Dorsal (above)
elongated wings

long antennae

bright orange
upperside

narrow black
border

Ventral (below)
silvery white line

215

Ventral

Comments: The Ruddy Daggerwing is a resident of the Keys but is much more commonly encountered on the south Florida mainland. Males commonly perch on sunlit leaves or overhanging branches along forest trails, light gaps or hammock borders. Adults readily visit available flowers.

Ruddy Daggerwing
Marpesia petreus

Family/Subfamily: Brush-foots (Nymphalidae)/ Admirals and Relatives (Limenitidinae)

Wingspan: 3.0–3.8" (7.6–9.7 cm)

Above: bright orange with irregular wing edges, thin black stripes and dark borders; hindwing bears a long, slender, dagger-like tail

Below: pinkish brown with narrow dark line through the middle of both wings and distinct cream body

Sexes: similar, although females lighter with more extensive dark markings

Egg: pale yellow, laid singly on host leaves

Larva: bright orange and cream with dark blue lateral markings and four long black spines on the back; head bears two long, curved black horns

Larval Host Plants: Strangler Fig and Short-leaved Fig

Habitat: hardwood hammocks, hammock edges and adjacent open areas

Broods: multiple generations

Abundance: occasional; local

Compare: Question Mark (pg. 203) is smaller, lacks dorsal black stripes and is absent from south Florida.

Resident

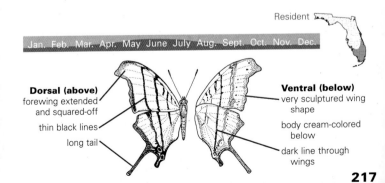

Jan. Feb. Mar. Apr. May June July Aug. Sept. Oct. Nov. Dec.

Dorsal (above)
forewing extended and squared-off

thin black lines

long tail

Ventral (below)
very sculptured wing shape

body cream-colored below

dark line through wings

217

Female

Ventral

Larva

Comments: The Monarch is undoubtedly the most familiar and widely recognized butterfly in North America. The species' annual fall mass migration is one of the greatest natural events undertaken by any organism on earth. Adults have a strong, soaring flight and it is an abundant garden visitor. The striped larvae feed on plants in the Milkweed family from which they sequester toxic chemicals that render them highly distasteful to certain predators. The adult butterflies advertise this unpalatability in dramatic fashion with their bold orange and black coloration.

Monarch
Danaus plexippus

Family/Subfamily: Brush-foots (Nymphalidae)/ Milkweed Butterflies (Danainae)

Wingspan: 3.5–4.0" (8.9–10.2 cm)

Above: orange with black veins and wing borders; black borders have two rows of small white spots; male has small black postmedian androconial scent patch on hindwing

Below: as above with lighter orange coloration

Sexes: similar; female lacks black scent patch

Egg: white, laid singly on host leaves

Larva: white with transverse black and yellow stripes; there is a pair of long, black filaments on each end

Larval Host Plants: various milkweed family plants including Mexican Milkweed, White Swamp Milkweed, Sandhill Milkweed and White Vine

Habitat: open, sunny locations including old fields, road-sides, pinelands, utility easements, sandhills, fallow agricultural land and gardens

Broods: multiple generations

Abundance: occasional to common

Compare: Queen (pg. 213) is smaller, tawny-orange in color and lacks black wing veins above. Gulf Fritillary (pg. 207) has elongated wings and prominent silver ventral spots.

Stray

Jan. Feb. Mar. Apr. May June July Aug. Sept. Oct. Nov. Dec.

male

Dorsal (above)
white spots
bright orange
two rows of white spots
black veins
scent patch on males only

Ventral (below)
lighter orange

Ventral

Larva

Comments: New data suggests that the once abundant
Common Checkered-Skipper has been almost entirely
displaced by the White Checkered-Skipper, which is
now the predominant species in Florida. Virtually iden-
tical in appearance and behavior, the two sibling
species can be reliably differentiated only through dis-
section. Adults have a rapid, darting flight and scurry
low over weedy vegetation. Although a nervous and
active species, individuals frequently stop to perch or
nectar. While at rest, adults generally hold their wings
wide open, making it easy to get a quick glimpse of
the butterfly's unique checkerboard pattern.

Common/White Checkered-Skipper
Pyrgus communis/Pyrgus albescens

Family/Subfamily: Skippers (Hesperiidae)/
Spread-wing Skippers (Pyrginae)

Wingspan: 0.75–1.25" (1.9–3.2 cm)

Above: male is black with numerous small, white spots
and some bluish white scaling on base of wings and
thorax; female is dark brown with reduced white scaling

Below: white with tan to brown irregular bands and
spots

Sexes: similar, although female has reduced white
markings

Egg: pale green, laid singly on host leaves

Larva: gray-green with dark dorsal stripe, light side
stripes and black head

Larval Host Plants: various mallow family plants
including Indian Hemp, Broomweed, Poppy Mallow
and False Mallow

Habitat: open, disturbed sites including roadsides, old
fields, utility easements and fallow agricultural land

Broods: multiple generations

Abundance: common

Compare: Tropical Checkered-Skipper (pg. 223) has
increased bluish white scaling on wings above and
diffuse ventral bands.

Resident

Jan. Feb. Mar. Apr. May June July Aug. Sept. Oct. Nov. Dec.

Dorsal (above)
fringe checkered to
apex

generally black and
white above

spots are much
smaller than those
in submarginal row

Ventral (below)
distinct bands

paler below

221

Male

Female   Ventral   Larva

Comments: The Tropical Checkered-Skipper is particularly abundant in late summer and early fall. Adults have
a fast, erratic flight and buzz rapidly among low vegetation, pausing occasionally to nectar or perch with their
wings outstretched. The light green larvae construct
individual shelters on the host by tying two or more
leaves together with silk.

Tropical Checkered-Skipper
Pyrgus oileus

Family/Subfamily: Skippers (Hesperiidae)/
Spread-wing Skippers (Pyrginae)

Wingspan: 0.90–1.35" (2.3–3.4 cm)

Above: male is dark blackish brown with numerous
small, white spots and extensive bluish gray hair-like
scales on base of wings and thorax; female is dark
brown with reduced white scaling

Below: powdery white with tan to brown irregular,
somewhat diffuse or smudged bands

Sexes: similar, although female darker with reduced
white markings

Egg: pale green, laid singly on host leaves

Larva: yellow-green with thin green dorsal stripe, light
side stripes and black head; body is covered with
numerous small, light-colored hairs

Larval Host Plants: various mallow family plants
including Indian Hemp, Broomweed and Poppy Mallow

Habitat: open, disturbed sites including roadsides, old
fields, utility easements and fallow agricultural land

Broods: multiple generations

Abundance: common to abundant

Compare: Common/White Checkered-Skipper (pg. 221)
has reduced bluish white scaling on wings above and
well-defined ventral bands.

Resident

Jan. Feb. Mar. Apr. May June July Aug. Sept. Oct. Nov. Dec.

male

Dorsal (above)
fringe dark toward
apex

long blue gray hair-
like scales

marginal spots
similar in size to
submarginal
spots

Ventral (below)
three dark spots along
leading margin

diffuse, smudged
bands

223

Summer

Winter pg. 240

Male

Larva

Comments: The Barred Sulphur is a common butterfly
of open, weedy sites throughout Florida, where it is
particularly abundant in the late summer and early fall.
Adults have a quick, dancing flight and typically bob
among low vegetation. Like many other sulphurs, the
butterfly displays dramatic seasonal variation in color
and behavior. Individuals produced during the summer
months are short-lived, reproductively active and
almost immaculate white beneath. Winter-forms have
highly pigmented and patterned ventral hindwings and
overwinter in reproductive diapause.

Barred Sulphur
Eurema daira

Family/Subfamily: Whites and Sulphurs (Pieridae)/ Sulphurs (Coliadinae)

Wingspan: 1.0–1.8" (2.5–4.6 cm)

Above: seasonally variable; winter-form bright yellow; summer-form whitish; all have black wing tips and a black bar along the trailing edge of forewing; forewing bar is diffuse or absent in female; wide black hindwing border is reduced to a small patch in winter-form

Below: seasonally variable; hindwings light gray to pure white in summer-form; tan to reddish brown with numerous pattern elements in winter-form

Sexes: similar, although black markings paler and less extensive in female

Egg: white, laid singly on host leaves

Larva: green with thin, lateral cream stripe

Larval Host Plants: Joint Vetch, Sandhill Joint Vetch, Pencilflower, Perennial Peanut and other Fabaceae

Habitat: open, disturbed sites including roadsides, pastures, utility easements and vacant fields

Broods: multiple generations; adults present year-round

Abundance: occasional to common

Compare: Dainty Sulphur (pg. 237) is much smaller and lacks white ventral hindwings. Little Sulphur (pg. 239) lacks black dorsal forewing bar.

Resident

Jan. Feb. Mar. Apr. May June July Aug. Sept. Oct. Nov. Dec.

male

Dorsal (above)
- black apex
- large black bar
- irregular black marginal patch or continuous border

Ventral (below)
- seasonally variable; immaculate white to patterned reddish brown

225

Male

Female Larva

Comments: A butterfly of dry, weedy sites, the Checkered White is a wide-ranging species but often only locally abundant. Adults have a fast, erratic flight and can be difficult to approach. The sexes differ dramatically and can be easily told apart even from a distance. Adults produced in early spring or late fall, under cooler conditions and shorter photoperiods, are typically smaller, darker and more heavily patterned.

Checkered White
Pontia protodice

Family/Subfamily: Whites and Sulphurs (Pieridae)/ Whites (Pierinae)

Wingspan: 1.25–2.00" (3.2–5.1 cm)

Above: male is white with charcoal markings on forewing and immaculate hindwing; female is grayish white with extensive black or grayish brown checkered markings on both wings

Below: hindwings white with grayish markings and yellow-green scaling along the veins; seasonally variable; cool season individuals are more heavily patterned

Sexes: similar, although female has more extensive black markings

Egg: yellow, laid singly on host leaves or flowers

Larva: gray with longitudinal yellow-orange stripe and black dots

Larval Host Plants: Virginia Pepper Grass

Habitat: open, disturbed sites including roadsides, pastures, utility easements, vacant fields, agricultural land

Broods: multiple generations

Abundance: occasional to common

Compare: Cabbage White (pg. 229) has charcoal wing tips and distinctive single or double dorsal forewing spots. Great Southern White (pg. 231) has scalloped black forewing border.

Resident

Jan. Feb. Mar. Apr. May June July Aug. Sept. Oct. Nov. Dec.

male

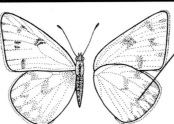

Dorsal (above)
white with black checkered pattern

Ventral (below)
seasonally variable; cool season forms are more heavily patterned

227

Larva

Comments: Accidentally introduced into the U.S. from Europe in 1860, the Cabbage White (or European Cabbage Butterfly) is one of the few butterfly species that is considered to be a serious agricultural and garden pest. Although extremely widespread and common, it is rarely encountered in southern portions of Florida and is often only locally abundant further north. Adults have a slow, somewhat awkward flight and are easy to observe. Although appearing pure white from a distance, upon closer inspection the wings beneath are delicately shaded with yellow.

Cabbage White
Pieris rapae

Family/Subfamily: Whites and Sulphurs (Pieridae)/
Whites (Pierinae)

Wingspan: 1.5–2.0" (3.8–5.1 cm)

Above: male is white with single black postmedian
forewing spot and wing tips; female is white with two
black postmedian forewing spots

Below: forewing white with two black spots and yellow
tips; hindwing immaculate whitish yellow

Sexes: similar, although female has two black spots on
forewing

Egg: white, laid singly on host leaves and flowers

Larva: green with small lateral yellow dashes and numerous short hairs

Larval Host Plants: cultivated and wild members of
the Mustard Family including Virginia Pepper Grass,
Wild Mustard, Wild Radish, broccoli and cabbage

Habitat: open, disturbed sites including roadsides, old
fields, utility easement, agricultural land and gardens

Broods: multiple generations

Abundance: occasional to common

Compare: Checkered White (pg. 227) lacks black tip on
forewing. Great Southern White (pg. 231) is larger and
has scalloped black forewing borders.

Resident

Jan. Feb. Mar. Apr. May June July Aug. Sept. Oct. Nov. Dec.

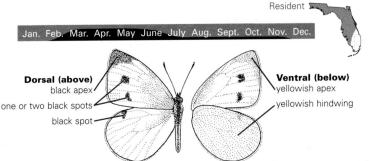

Dorsal (above)
black apex
one or two black spots
black spot

Ventral (below)
yellowish apex
yellowish hindwing

229

Male

Female

Larva

Comments: The Great Southern White's antennae have a distinctive blue tip. While males are always white, females may be white, gray or an intermediate color. Adults have a low, generally casual flight. The butterfly occasionally experiences tremendous population outbreaks. Extensive northward movements of adults along the coast often follow such explosions in number.

Great Southern White
Ascia monuste

Family/Subfamily: Whites and Sulphurs (Pieridae)/ Whites (Pierinae)

Wingspan: 1.5–2.5" (3.8–6.4 cm)

Above: male is immaculate white with narrow, black scalloped forewing border; female is seasonally variable; dirty white to gray with more pronounced black forewing border and black forewing cell spot

Below: males white with pale yellow hindwings; females dirty white to gray

Sexes: similar, although female has more gray scaling and a single black dorsal forewing spot

Egg: yellow, laid singly or in small groups on host leaves

Larva: yellow with grayish purple longitudinal stripes, black dots and numerous small hairs

Larval Host Plants: Virginia Pepper Grass, Saltwort, Sea Rocket and others

Habitat: open sites including roadsides, coastal dunes, salt marshes, vacant fields, agricultural land

Broods: multiple generations

Abundance: occasional to common

Compare: Cabbage White (pg. 229) is smaller and lacks black scalloped forewing border. Florida White (pg. 233) lacks black scalloped forewing border.

Resident

Jan. Feb. Mar. Apr. May June July Aug. Sept. Oct. Nov. Dec.

Dorsal (above)
narrow, scalloped
black border
blue tips

Ventral (below)

Male

Comments: The Florida White is restricted to the confines of south Florida's tropical hardwood hammocks. Males have a fast, erratic flight and actively patrol sunlit openings and forest canopies for females. This butterfly regularly undergoes dramatic fluctuations in population numbers, being extremely abundant in certain years or highly localized and rare in others. During times of increased population abundance, the adults may wander extensively throughout the Florida peninsula. Adults can be seen during all months of the year in Florida.

Florida White
Appias drusilla

Family/Subfamily: Whites and Sulphurs (Pieridae)/ Whites (Pierinae)

Wingspan: 1.6–2.4" (4.1–6.1 cm)

Above: narrow, somewhat elongated forewings; male is immaculate white with narrow black scaling along forewing costal margin; female is white with black wing tip, outer margin and costal margin; hindwings white to pale yellow

Below: white with with yellowish orange basal scaling

Sexes: similar, although female has increased black markings

Egg: yellow, laid singly on the new growth of host

Larva: greenish blue with numerous small, yellow dots and two short tails

Larval Host Plants: Milkbark, Guiana Plum and Limber Caper

Habitat: tropical hardwood hammocks and adjacent open areas

Broods: multiple generations

Abundance: occasional

Compare: Similar in size to Great Southern White (pg. 231) but has more prominently pointed wings and lacks black scalloped forewing border.

Resident

| Jan. | Feb. | Mar. | Apr. | May | June | July | Aug. | Sept. | Oct. | Nov. | Dec. |

male

Dorsal (above)
black apex (female only)

black outer margin (female only)

unmarked white wing (male only)

Ventral (below)
yellowish orange basal coloring

233

Ventral

Comments: The White Peacock, although widespread, is often somewhat local in occurrence. Adults have a fast, erratic flight usually within a few feet of the ground and readily alight on low vegetation. They avidly visit available flowers. Adults can be found year-round in south Florida.

White Peacock
Anartia jatrophae

Family/Subfamily: Brush-foots (Nymphalidae)/
True Brush-foots (Nymphalinae)

Wingspan: 2.0–2.5" (5.1–6.4 cm)

Above: white with dark brown marking and dull orange
scaling along wing margins; forewing has a single
black spot; hindwing has a short, stubby tail and two
black postmedian spots

Below: as above with paler brown wing margins and
pinkish markings

Sexes: similar, though female is larger and has broader
wings

Egg: green, laid singly on host leaves

Larva: charcoal gray with small silvery-white spots and
black, branched spines

Larval Host Plants: Frogfruit and Water Hyssop

Habitat: open, disturbed sites including wet ditches,
roadsides, pond edges, old fields and gardens

Broods: multiple generations

Abundance: common

Compare: unique

Resident Stray

Jan. Feb. Mar. Apr. May June July Aug. Sept. Oct. Nov. Dec.

Dorsal (above)
orange margin
black spot
black spots
short, stubby tail

Ventral (below)

Male

Larva

Comments: As its name implies, the Dainty Sulphur is Florida's smallest yellow butterfly. It flies low among the vegetation and is easily overlooked. It is common throughout the year in southern portions of the state but less numerous and often quite local in occurrence further north. Adults regularly congregate at damp ground.

Dainty Sulphur
Nathalis iole

Family/Subfamily: Whites and Sulphurs (Pieridae)/
Sulphurs (Coliadinae)

Wingspan: 0.75–1.25" (1.9–3.2 cm)

Above: lemon yellow with black forewing tip and black
bar along trailing edge of forewing; female has orange-
yellow hindwings with more extensive black markings

Below: hindwings yellow with greenish markings; seasonally variable; winter-form more heavily pigmented

Sexes: similar, although black markings more extensive
on female

Egg: yellow, laid singly on host leaves

Larva: green with thin, lateral yellow and lavender stripes

Larval Host Plants: Spanish Needles

Habitat: open, disturbed sites including roadsides, pastures, utility easements, vacant fields, agricultural land
and canal banks

Broods: multiple generations

Abundance: occasional to common

Compare: Barred Sulphur (pg. 241) is larger with white
ventral hindwings.

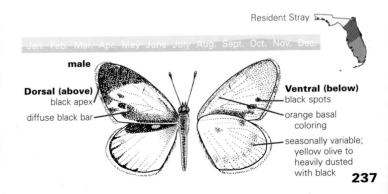

Resident Stray

Jan. Feb. Mar. Apr. May June July Aug. Sept. Oct. Nov. Dec.

male

Dorsal (above)
black apex
diffuse black bar

Ventral (below)
black spots
orange basal
coloring
seasonally variable;
yellow olive to
heavily dusted
with black

237

Male

Female

Larva

Comments: The Little Sulphur has a low, darting flight and an affinity for dry, open habitats. Although found throughout the year in Florida, it is particularly abundant in the late summer and early fall. Like other members of the genus, it produces different seasonal forms that vary in coloration, behavior and reproductive activity.

Little Sulphur
Eurema lisa

Family/Subfamily: Whites and Sulphurs (Pieridae)/ Sulphurs (Coliadinae)

Wingspan: 1.0–1.6" (2.5–4.1 cm)

Above: bright yellow with black forewing tip and narrow black wing borders; female pale yellow to near white with lighter black markings

Below: seasonally variable; hindwings yellow to near white with pinkish red spot in upper margin; winter-form darker yellow with additional pattern elements and pink wing fringe

Sexes: similar, although markings and color paler on female

Egg: white, laid singly on host leaves

Larva: green with thin, lateral cream-white stripe

Larval Host Plants: primarily Partridge Pea and Sensitive Pea

Habitat: open, disturbed sites including roadsides, pastures, utility easements, vacant fields, agricultural land and open sandhills

Abundance: occasional to common

Compare: Superficially resembles Dainty Sulphur (pg. 237) and Barred Sulphur (pg. 241) but lacks black dorsal forewing bar.

Resident

Jan. Feb. Mar. Apr. May June July Aug. Sept. Oct. Nov. Dec.

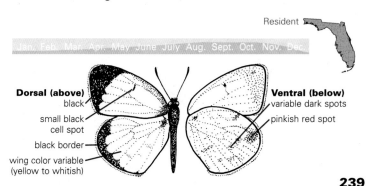

Dorsal (above)
black
small black cell spot
black border
wing color variable (yellow to whitish)

Ventral (below)
variable dark spots
pinkish red spot

239

Male

Summer pg. 224   Winter   Larva

Comments: The Barred Sulphur is a common butterfly of open, weedy sites throughout Florida, where it is particularly abundant in the late summer and early fall. Adults have a quick, dancing flight and typically bob among low vegetation. Like many other sulphurs, the butterfly displays dramatic seasonal variation in color and behavior. Individuals produced during the summer months are short-lived, reproductively active and almost immaculate white beneath. Winter-forms have highly pigmented and patterned ventral hindwings and overwinter in reproductive diapause.

Barred Sulphur
Eurema daira

Family/Subfamily: Whites and Sulphurs (Pieridae)/ Sulphurs (Coliadinae)

Wingspan: 1.0–1.8" (2.5–4.6 cm)

Above: seasonally variable; winter-form bright yellow; summer-form whitish; all have black wing tips and a black bar along the trailing edge of forewing; forewing bar is diffuse or absent in female; wide black hindwing border is reduced to a small patch in winter-form

Below: seasonally variable; hindwings light gray to pure white in summer-form; tan to reddish brown with numerous pattern elements in winter-form

Sexes: similar, although black markings paler and less extensive in female

Egg: white, laid singly on host leaves

Larva: green with thin, lateral cream stripe

Larval Host Plants: Joint Vetch, Sandhill Joint Vetch, Pencilflower, Perennial Peanut and other Fabaceae

Habitat: open, disturbed sites including roadsides, pastures, utility easements and vacant fields

Broods: multiple generations; adults present year-round

Abundance: occasional to common

Compare: Dainty Sulphur (pg. 237) is much smaller and lacks white ventral hindwings. Little Sulphur (pg. 239) lacks black dorsal forewing bar.

Resident

Jan. Feb. Mar. Apr. May June July Aug. Sept. Oct. Nov. Dec.

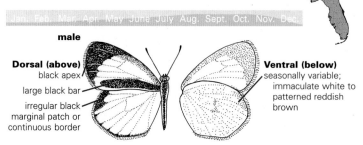

male

Dorsal (above)
black apex
large black bar
irregular black marginal patch or continuous border

Ventral (below)
seasonally variable; immaculate white to patterned reddish brown

Winter

Larva

Comments: The only Florida sulphur with pointed
forewings, the Dogface is a medium-sized butterfly
with a powerful, rapid flight. It is named after the
unique pattern formed by the black and yellow markings on the wings above that resemble (with some
imagination) the head of a dog in profile. Adults display
considerable seasonal variation. Winter-forms are particularly stunning with rich pink scaling on the wings
beneath. They overwinter in reproductive diapause.

Southern Dogface
Zerene cesonia

Family/Subfamily: Whites and Sulphurs (Pieridae)/ Sulphurs (Coliadinae)

Wingspan: 1.9–2.5" (4.8–6.4 cm)

Above: yellow with broad, black forewing margin highly scalloped to form image of dog's head in profile; forewing pointed with single back cell spot and increased black scaling on basal area; hindwing has narrow black margin

Below: hindwings seasonally variable; summer-form is yellow with two small silver spots; winter-form has increased rosy-pink scaling

Sexes: similar, although black markings duller and less extensive on female

Egg: white, laid singly on host leaves

Larva: varies; plain green to green with orange lateral stripe and transverse black and yellow stripes

Larval Host Plants: False Indigo, Summer Farewell

Habitat: open, dry sites including pineland, oak scrub, fields and roadsides

Broods: multiple generations; adults may be found year-round

Abundance: occasional

Compare: Cloudless Sulphur (pg. 245) lacks black markings and pointed forewings.

Resident

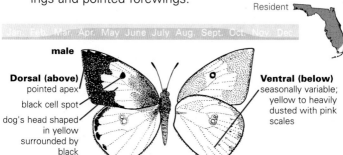

Jan. Feb. Mar. Apr. May June July Aug. Sept. Oct. Nov. Dec.

male

Dorsal (above)
pointed apex

black cell spot

dog's head shaped in yellow surrounded by black

Ventral (below)
seasonally variable; yellow to heavily dusted with pink scales

243

Male

Female Larva

Comments: The Cloudless Sulphur is a large yellow butterfly with a fast, powerful flight. Abundant throughout
the Southeast, it is a common garden visitor and one
of the most easily recognized butterflies in Florida.
Adults have an extremely long proboscis and can feed
at many long, tubular flowers typically inaccessible to
other butterflies. Fall individuals undergo a massive,
southward migration into Florida to overwinter. The
annual event is one of the sunshine state's most
impressive natural phenomena.

Cloudless Sulphur
Phoebis sennae

Family/Subfamily: Whites and Sulphurs (Pieridae)/ Sulphurs (Coliadinae)

Wingspan: 2.2–2.8" (5.6–7.1 cm)

Above: bright lemon yellow; female has broken black wing borders and hollow black forewing spot

Below: male is greenish yellow with virtually no markings; female is yellow with pinkish brown markings and several small silver spots in center of each wing; seasonally variable; winter-form adults more heavily marked

Sexes: similar, although female more heavily marked

Egg: white, laid singly on host leaves or flower buds

Larva: green or yellow with broad lateral yellow stripe marked with blue spots or transverse bands

Larval Host Plants: various wild and ornamental Cassia species including Partridge Pea, Sensitive Pea, Sicklepod Senna, Christmas Senna and Candle Plant

Habitat: open, disturbed sites including roadsides, vacant fields, agricultural land, parks and home gardens

Broods: multiple generations

Abundance: common to abundant

Compare: Orange-Barred Sulphur (pg. 247) male has orange dorsal forewing bar. Female has submarginal row of dark spots on forewing above.

Resident

Jan. Feb. Mar. Apr. May June July Aug. Sept. Oct. Nov. Dec.

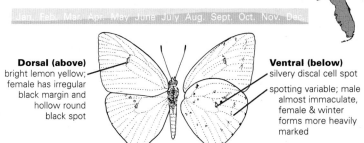

Dorsal (above)
bright lemon yellow; female has irregular black margin and hollow round black spot

Ventral (below)
silvery discal cell spot

spotting variable; male almost immaculate, female & winter forms more heavily marked

245

Male

Female   Larva

Comments: Named for its distinct orange forewing band in males, the Orange-barred Sulphur is a large yellow butterfly with a strong and rapid flight. Found year-round in south Florida, it regularly moves northward each year to temporarily colonize additional portions of the peninsula. It is rare or absent from the panhandle. Unlike many butterfly species, it is at home in more urban locations were its ornamental larval hosts commonly occur. The butterfly became established in Florida sometime during the late 1920s and has become an abundant resident.

Orange-barred Sulphur
Phoebis philea

Family/Subfamily: Whites and Sulphurs (Pieridae)/ Sulphurs (Coliadinae)

Wingspan: 2.75–3.40" (7.0–8.6 cm)

Above: male is bright yellow with wide orange forewing bar and orange scaling along hindwing border; summer-form female is pale white-yellow with narrow dark wing borders; winter-form female is yellow with wide orange band along trailing edge of hindwing; forewing has broken submarginal band

Below: male is bright yellow with small dark spots; summer-form female is orange yellow with fine dark mottling; winter-form female has increased markings

Sexes: dissimilar; female seasonally variable

Egg: white, laid singly on host leaves

Larva: green-yellow with a black lateral stripe and numerous black points

Larval Host Plants: various woody sennas including Candle Plant, Bahana Senna and Christmas Senna

Habitat: open, disturbed sites and urban areas

Broods: multiple generations; all year in south Florida

Abundance: occasional to common

Compare: Cloudless Sulphur (pg. 245) is smaller and lighter yellow. Large Orange Sulphur (pg. 201) has unbroken diagonal line on ventral forewing.

Resident Stray

Jan. Feb. Mar. Apr. May June July Aug. Sept. Oct. Nov. Dec.

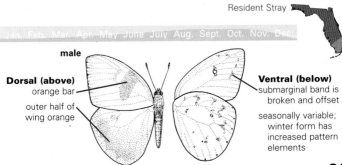

male

Dorsal (above)
orange bar
outer half of wing orange

Ventral (below)
submarginal band is broken and offset

seasonally variable; winter form has increased pattern elements

Male

Dark-form female
pg. 60

Female

Larva

Comments: Easily recognized by its bold, black stripes and yellow wings, the Tiger Swallowtail is one of the state's most familiar butterflies. Adults have a strong, agile flight and often soar high in the treetops. A common and conspicuous garden visitor, adults are readily drawn to available flowers. Males often congregate in large numbers at mud puddles or moist ground. Dark-form females mimic the toxic Pipevine Swallowtail to gain protection from predators.

Eastern Tiger Swallowtail
Papilio glaucus

Family/Subfamily: Swallowtails (Papilionidae)/ Swallowtails (Papilioninae)

Wingspan: 3.5–5.5" (8.9–14.0 cm)

Above: yellow with black forewing stripes and broad black wing margins; single row of yellow spots along outer edge of each wing

Below: yellow with black stripes and black wing margins; hindwing margins have increased blue scaling and a single submarginal row of yellow-orange, crescent-shaped spots; abdomen yellow with black stripes

Sexes: dissimilar; male always yellow but females have two color forms; yellow female has increased blue scaling in black hindwing border; dark-form female is mostly black with extensive blue hindwing markings

Egg: green, laid singly on upper surface of host leaves

Larva: green; enlarged thorax and two small false eyespots

Larval Host Plants: Wild Cherry, White Ash and Sweet Bay

Habitat: mixed forests, wooded swamps, hammocks, forest edges, suburban gardens

Broods: multiple generations

Abundance: occasional to common

Compare: Yellow-form unique. Pipevine Swallowtail (pg. 53) is much smaller.

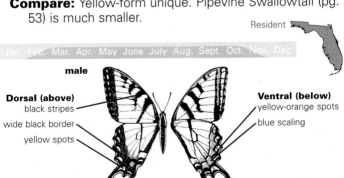

Resident

Jan. Feb. Mar. Apr. May June July Aug. Sept. Oct. Nov. Dec.

male

Dorsal (above)
black stripes
wide black border
yellow spots

Ventral (below)
yellow-orange spots
blue scaling

PLANTS FOR YOUR BUTTERFLY GARDEN

The following are some recommended adult nectar sources and larval hosts for a Florida butterfly garden. Most of the species are readily available at most retail garden centers or native plant nurseries. Before purchasing any landscape plant, always inquire with your local nursery personnel as to the specific soil, light, and care requirements needed for optimal growth and maintenance. Additionally, it is also a good idea to understand the plant's growth habit and eventual size at maturity before placing it in the ground. Visit a demonstration garden, a neighbor's yard or a nearby botanical garden to see how the plant looks after it has had a chance to grow a bit. Finally, remember that pesticides are not recommended for any butterfly garden as they can harm the very organisms you wish to attract. Consider using beneficial insects or insecticidal soap first before resorting to more extreme measures. If pesticides are required, always treat pest problems on a local level by applying treatment only to the infested plant and being careful of drift to neighboring vegetation.

Adult Nectar Sources

Herbaceous Perennials

Mexican Milkweed (*Asclepias curassavica*)

White Swamp Milkweed (*Asclepias perennis*)

Butterfly Weed (*Asclepias tuberosa*)

Carolina Aster (*Aster caroliniana*)

Spanish Needles (*Bidens alba*)

Florida Paint Brush (*Carphephorus corymbosus*)

Glorybower (*Clerodendron bungei*)

False Heather (*Cuphea hyssopifolia*)

Mist Flower (*Eupatorium coelestinum*)

Joe-pye Weed (*Eupatorium fistulosum*)

Indian Blanket (*Gaillardia pulchella*)

Moss Verbena (*Glandularia pulchella*)

Creeping Heliotrope (*Heliotropium amplexicaule*)

Lantana (*Lantana camara*)

Purple Weeping Lantana (*Lantana montevidensis*)

blazing star (*Liatris spp.*)

Scarlet Beebalm (*Monarda didyma*)

Horse Mint (*Monarda punctata*)

Fire Spike (*Odontonema strictum*)

Drummond Phlox (*Phlox drummondii*)

Frogfruit (*Phylla nodiflora*)

Pickerelweed (*Pontederia cordata*)

mountain mint (*Pycnanthemum spp.*)

Autumn Sage (*Salvia gregii*)

Mexican Sage (*Salvia leucantha*)

sedum (*Sedum spp.*)

goldenrod (*Solidago spp.*)

Stokes Aster (*Stokesia laevis*)

Tall Verbena (*Verbena bonariensis*)

ironweed (*Vernonia spp.*)

Shrubs and Trees

Glossy Abelia *(Abelia x grandiflora)*
Red Buckeye *(Aesculus pavia)*
Silktree *(Albizia julibrissin)*
False Indigo *(Amorpha fruticosa)*
Butterfly Bush *(Buddlea davidii)*
Pride of Barbados *(Caesalpina pulcherima)*
Bluebeard *(Caryopteris x chandonensis)*
New Jersey Tea *(Ceanothus americanus)*
Buttonbush *(Cephalanthus occidentalis)*
Redbud *(Cercis canadensis)*
Sweet Pepperbush *(Clethra alnifolia)*

Firebush *(Hamelia patens)*
hibiscus *(Hibiscus spp.)*
Dahoon Holly *(Ilex cassine)*
Yaupon Holly *(Ilex vomitoria)*
Virginia Willow *(Itea virginica)*
Chickasaw Plum *(Prunus angustifolia)*
Black Cherry *(Prunus serotina)*
Hog Plum *(Prunus umbellata)*
Wild Coffee *(Psychotria nervosa)*
Wild Azalea *(Rhododendron canescens)*
Blue Porterweed *(Stachytarpheta urticifolia)*
Sweet Viburnum *(Viburnum odoratissimum)*
Chaste Tree *(Vitex agnus-castus)*

Vines

Coral Vine *(Antigon leptopus)*
Bougainvillea *(Bougainvillea glabra)*
morning glory *(Ipomoea spp.)*

Climbing Hempweed *(Mikania scandens)*
Maypop *(Passiflora incarnata)*
Flame Vine *(Senecio confuses)*

Annuals

Ageratum *(Ageratum houstonianum)*
Spider Plant *(Cleome hasslerana)*
Dianthus *(Dianthus chinensis)*
Globe Amaranth *(Gomphrena globosa)*
impatiens *(Impatiens spp.)*
Sweet Alyssum *(Lobularia maritima)*

Flowering Tobacco *(Nicotiana alata)*
Pentas *(Pentas lanceolata)*
Drummond Phlox *(Phlox drummondii)*
Tropical Sage *(Salvia coccinea)*
Mexican sunflower *(Tithonia spp.)*
Verbena *(Verbena X hybrida)*
Zinnia *(Zinnia elegans)*

Larval Host Plants

Alfalfa *(Medicago sativa)*
Amaranth, Spiny *(Amaranthus spinosus)*
Ash, Wafer *(Ptelea trifoliata)*
Ash, White *(Fraxinus americana)*
Aster, Bushy *(Aster dumosus)*
Aster, Frost *(Aster pilosus)*
asters *(Aster spp.)*
Balloon Vine *(Cardiospermum halicababum)*
Bay, Red *(Persea borbonia)*

Bay, Silk *(Persea humilis)*
Bay, Swamp *(Persea palustris)*
Bay, Sweet *(Magnolia virginiana)*
beggarweeds *(Desmodium spp.)*
Blackbead *(Pithecellobium keyense)*
bluestems *(Andropogon spp.)*
Broomweed *(Sida acuta)*
Camphor-tree *(Cinnamomum camphora)*
Candle Plant *(Cassia alata)*
Cane, Giant *(Arundinaria gigantea)*

cannas (Canna spp.)

Caper, Limber (Capparis flexuosa)

carrot family (Apiaceae) includes dill, fennel and parsley

Cassia species (Cassia spp.)

Cat's Claw (Pithecellobium unguis-cati)

Cedar, Southern Red (Juniperus silicicola)

Cherry, Black (Prunus virginiana)

Cherry, Wild (Prunus serotina)

Clover, White (Trifolium repens)

Clover, White Sweet (Melilotus alba)

clovers (Trifolium spp.)

clovers, bush (Lespedeza spp.)

Coontie (Zamia pumila)

Crabgrass, Hairy (Digitaria sanguinalis)

Crabgrass, Shaggy (Digitaria villosa)

Croton, Silver (Croton argyranthemus)

Croton, Woolly (Croton linearis)

Cudweed, Purple (Gnaphalium purpureum)

Cudweed, Narrow-leaved (Gnaphalium falcatum)

Cudweed, Wandering (Gnaphalium pensylvanicum)

dogwoods (Cornus spp.)

Elm, American (Ulmus americana)

Elm, Winged (Ulmus alata)

Fig, Short-leaved (Ficus citrifolia)

Fig, Strangler (Ficus aurea)

foxglove, false (Agalinus spp.)

Frogfruit (Phyla nodiflora)

glasswort (Salicornia spp.)

Grass, Bermuda (Cynodon dactylon)

Grass, Purpletop (Tridens flavus)

Grass, Salt (Distichlis spicata)

Grass, St. Augustine (Stenotaphrum secundatum)

Grass, Switch (Panicum virgatum)

Grass, Virginia Pepper (Lepidium virginicum)

grasses (Poaceae)

Green Shrimp Plant (Blechum brownei)

Hackberry, Common (Celtis occidentalis)

hawthorn (Crataegus spp.)

Hemp, Indian (Sida rhombifolia)

Hercules Club (Zanthoxylum clava-hercules)

hickories (Carya spp.)

Holly, American (Ilex opaca)

Holly, Dahoon (Ilex cassine)

Holly, Yaupon (Ilex vomitoria)

Hyssop, Water (Bacopa monnieri)

Indigo, Creeping (Indigofera spicata)

Indigo, False (Amorpha fruticosa)

Indigo, Hairy (Indigofera hirsuta)

Kudzu (Pueraria lobata)

Lamb's Quarters (Chenopidium album)

Leadwort (Plumbago auriculata)

legumes (Fabaceae)

Lime, Wild (Zanthoxylum fagara)

lovegrass (Eragrostis spp.)

mallow family (Malvaceae spp.)

Mallow, False (Malvasreum corchorifolium)

Mallow, Poppy (Callirhoe papaver)

Mango (Mangifera indica)

Mangrove, Black (Avicennia germinans)

Mangrove, Red (Rhizophora mangle)

Maypop (Passiflora incarnata –passionflower)

milk peas (Galactia spp.)

Milkbark (Drypetes diversifolia)

milkweed family (Asclepias spp.)

Milkweed, Mexican (Asclepias currasavica)

Milkweed, Sandhill (Asclepias humistrata)

Milkweed, White Swamp (Asclepias perennis)

Mistletoe (Phoradendron serotinum)

mustard family (Brassicaceae)

Mustard, Wild (Brassica campestris)

Myrtle, Wax (Myrica cerifera)

Nettle, False (Boehmeria cylindrica)

nettles (Urtica spp.)
nickerbean (Caesalpinia spp.)
Oak, Black (Quercus velutina)
Oak, Live (Quercus virginiana)
Oak, Myrtle (Quercus myrtifolia)
Oak, Post (Quercus stellata)
Oak, Turkey (Quercus laevis)
Oak, Water (Quercus nigra)
Oak, White (Quercus alba)
oaks (Quercus spp.)
panic grasses (Panicum spp.)
Paspalum, Rustyseed (Paspalum langei)
Passion Flower, Corky-stemmed (Passiflora suberosa)
Passion Flower, Many-flowered (Passiflora multiflora)
Passion Flower, Yellow (Passiflora lutea)
passion flowers (Passiflora spp.)
pawpaws (Asimina spp.)
Pea, Butterfly (Clitoria mariana)
Pea, Partridge (Cassia fasciculata)
Pea, Sensitive (Cassia nictitans)
Peanut, Hog (Amphicarpa bracteata)
Peanut, Perennial (Arachis glabrata)
Pellitory (Parietaria floridana)
Pencilflower (Stylosanthes biflora)
Pipevine, Elegant (Aristolochia elegans)
pipevines (Aristolochia spp.)
plantain (Plantago spp.)
Plum, Guiana (Drypetes lateriflora)
Plumbago, Wild (Plumbago scandens)
Radish, Wild (Raphanus raphanistrum)
Redbud (Cercis canadensis)
Saltwort (Batis maritima)
Sand Vine (Cynanchum angustifolium)
Sassafras (Sassafras albidum)
Sawgrass (Cladium jamaicense)
Sea Rocket (Cakile lanceolata)
sedges (Carex spp.)
Senna, Bahana (Cassia chapmanii)

Senna, Christmas (Cassia bicapsularis)
Senna, Coffee (Cassia occidentalis)
Senna, Sicklepod (Cassia obtusifolia)
Sida (Sida acuta)
Snakeroot, Virginia (Aristolochia serpentaria)
Southern Cutgrass (Leersia hexandra)
Spanish Needles (Bidens alba)
Sparkleberry (Vaccinium arboreum)
Spicebush (Lindera benzoin)
Sugarberry (Celtis laevigata)
sumac (Rhus spp.)
Sumac, Winged (Rhus copallina)
Summer Farewell (Dalea pinnata)
Sweet Everlasting (Gnaphalium obtusifolium)
Tamarind, Wild (Lysiloma latisiliquum)
Tea, Mexican (Chenopidium ambrosiodes)
Tea, New Jersey (Ceanothus americana)
Thistle, Yellow (Cirsium horridulum)
thistles (Cirsium spp.)
toadflax (Linaria spp.)
Torchwood (Amyris elemifera)
twinflower (Dyschoriste spp.)
vegetables (broccoli, cabbage and others)
Vetch, Joint (Aeschyomene americana)
vetch, milk (Astragalus spp.)
Vetch, Sandhill Joint (Aeschyomene viscidula)
violets (Viola spp.)
White Vine (Sarcostemma clausum)
Willow, Black (Salix nigra)
Willow, Coastal Plain (Salix caroliniana)
Willow, Weeping (Salix babylonica)
wisterias (Wisteria spp.)
yuccas (Yucca spp.)

CHECKLIST/INDEX

Use the boxes to check the butterflies you've seen.

ABOUT THE AUTHOR

Jaret C. Daniels, Ph.D., is a professional nature photographer and entomologist specializing in the ecology and conservation biology of Lepidoptera. He has authored numerous scientific papers, popular articles and books on butterflies, insects, wildlife conservation and butterfly gardening. He currently lives in Gainesville, Florida, with his wife Stephanie.